cursed by a happy childhood

cursed

by a

happy childhood

Tales of Growing Up,
Then and Now

CARL LENNERTZ

Harmony Books
NEW YORK

Published by Harmony Books, New York, New York.
Member of the Crown Publishing Group,
a division of Random House, Inc.
www.crownpublishing.com

HARMONY BOOKS is a registered trademark and the
Harmony Books colophon is a trademark of
Random House, Inc.

Printed in the United States of America

DESIGN BY LYNNE AMFT

Library of Congress Cataloging-in-Publication Data
Lennertz, Carl.
Cursed by a happy childhood : tales of growing up, then and now /
Carl Lennertz.—1st ed.
1. Lennertz, Carl—Childhood and youth. 2. Long Island (N.Y.)—
Social life and customs. 3. Long Island (N.Y.)—Biography. I. Title.
F127.L8L46   2004
974.7'25—dc22   2003023390

ISBN 1-4000-5045-6

10 9 8 7 6 5 4 3 2 1

First Edition

To all the doctors of the world, but especially

DR. CYNTHIA KRAUSE,

who safely delivered our daughter into this world;

DR. ALAN ATKINS,

who helped me sort out the confusion of fatherhood;

and, of course,

DR. SEUSS,

who gave parents and kids everywhere hours of

reading pleasure together.

Some luck lies in not getting what you thought you wanted

but getting what you have, which once you have got it

you may be smart enough to see is what you would have

wanted had you known.

GARRISON KEILLOR

Contents

contents

* x *

contents

contents

contents

contents

To My Fellow Parents

THIS BOOK BEGAN AS A DIARY I STARTED TO KEEP
for my eleven-year-old daughter.

She was two years away from a birthday with "teen" in
it, so I felt the time was right to put down on paper some
thoughts and advice that might be of use to her in the future.
I started with some important things that were happening in
her life, and then if it applied, I'd make a connection to a
good memory from my childhood and teen years. Everything I planned to record was something we'd either talked
about already or would when the time arose, but I felt a
strong need to get it all down in one place.

Was I really writing this in order to pass along some supposed wisdom to her, or was I doing it for myself? Were
things just happening so fast that I felt a need to take time
out to look back as well as anticipate what lay ahead?
(There's an idea: time-outs for parents.)

A beautifully bound journal that had long been awaiting

use (where does the time go?) was soon filled with a stream of reflections. I hadn't handwritten so many pages since the long-ago college days of earnest ten-page letters to a faraway friend or girlfriend, but I had tapped a reservoir of wonderful recollections about my rural upbringing. There was so much I wanted to say, but I worried that my adolescence might not be relevant, that it was just too different a place and time. Me: *boy/small town/1960s*. Her: *girl/big city/2002 and counting*. But I was surprised, pleasantly so, at what I found as I wrote.

It has been nearly a dozen years of parental learning on the job for my wife and me, and what did we know going in? Teachers must have degrees, but parents are "graduated" with a hodgepodge of well-meaning advice and a few books by experts from divergent schools of thought. Since parenting often feels like one *huge* essay question without real grades, I wanted to try and take some sort of measure of how I'd done so far. I knew I'd find room for improvement, but just how much? Most of the time, being a parent, I have felt like the manic man on *The Ed Sullivan Show* spinning all those plates on the ends of poles—and mine, of course, were often very, very wobbly. My wife seemed much more secure in her parenting style, while I felt thoroughly confused most of the time.

I wrote for a little bit each weekend over the course of a year, and found that I had much I wanted to share with other graduates of the "School for Imperfect Parents." We are all so anxious to raise great kids, and yes, we can always be better at it, but we learn as we go along, especially if we reflect on our past and then let ourselves be taught by the very ones we are trying to guide, our children.

I'm no parenting expert, but I was a kid once, so here goes.

CARL LENNERTZ
NEW YORK CITY, 2003

cursed by a happy childhood

PENNY LANE

(John Lennon-Paul McCartney)

Capitol
RECORDS

Maclen
Music, Inc.
BMI-3:00
5810
(45-X45871)
Produced in
England by
George Martin

THE BEATLES

music and memory

MY DAUGHTER IS ACROSS THE ROOM READING A pop music magazine, her legs tucked up under her little girl's body in an armchair.

It is strangely reassuring to me that such magazines still exist. While celebrity-watching is now officially out of control in our culture, a kid can still have innocent fun talking with friends about the latest singers. And it isn't just blind idolatry. If one of their favorites gets too grown-up or stuck-up, my daughter and her friends start to tune out. But ultimately, it is still the music itself that matters most. Does a song sound good? Do its words and rhythm catch in a kid's head and heart, just as it had to for us?

I'm happy that she has her own music, yet still tolerates my occasional attempts to play some of my music for her. If it has a strong beat and good harmonies, chances are she'll like it. The Beatles, the Beach Boys, Santana, and Sting all became mutual favorites. (And, I confess, we both dig a little disco, too.) My well-intentioned dad tried to get us kids to listen to opera and, failing that, Broadway tunes. It just wasn't "cool," so we kids did our best to make an excuse to leave the room. (Got lots of homework, Dad!) Also, I just couldn't suspend belief when actors broke out into song in the middle of Main Street. I don't know if I was being too literal or just contrary.

Later in life I did come to appreciate music that was more intricate than a three-minute pop song (rock operas, anyone?) and to thoroughly enjoy musicals and the art of putting serious themes to music. Still, when it was my turn to "inflict" music on an offspring, I had to remind myself that each of us has to come to accept certain aspects of culture at our own speed. In other words, I shouldn't let my adult feelings get hurt when my daughter gives the thumbs-down to an icon from my youth.

For teens in the late 1960s, music was an integral part of friendship. Every Tuesday night my best friend and I would listen to the Top Twenty Countdown as we did our homework in our respective homes. We would call each other at the commercial breaks to talk about the newest songs and to guess what was going to go "all the way to #1."

It didn't matter that the radio signal barely reached us way out in our small town, a hundred miles from the New York City AM station we adored. Much more so than now, the radio was our connection to the rest of the world and to what was happening in music, whether it was folk, rock, or soul. Our little radios were like portals, and the music that poured out was "ours," not our parents'. The songs—whether about love or politics or personal freedom—made us feel rebellious, but mostly they just sounded good to us.

My friend and I marveled at the DJ's uncanny ability to talk into the beginning of the song, ending his verbal riff at the exact moment the singer began. (Is he going to make it, did he cut it too close—ohhhh, just in time!) We imagined a room somewhere in the city packed floor to ceiling with 45s. We couldn't figure out why British guys lost their accents when they sang, and we didn't know then that the Supremes didn't get along. It only mattered that we were up on the latest hits. I used to list the top twenty song titles in a notebook, keeping a chart from week to week. (Then as now, list-making gave me a brief sense of control and accomplishment, a sense of everything being in its place in my little corner of the world—at least for a short while.)

A mark of maturity for a kid back then was the transition from singles to albums. Singles = junior high school; albums = high school and college. I squeezed in a *lot* of album-listening time, either fully engrossed in each song and its lyrics, or letting an album be a sound track to my daily life. All these years later I still anticipate the first notes of the next song on any album I owned then. Call it musical déjà vu.

My daughter and I share the thrill of buying records. I bought my first one—a Beatles album, of course—at my local hardware store, as my hometown wasn't big enough for a record shop. Other rural kids might have found their first records at a Woolworth's or the grocery store, but for me, heaven was Rothman's Hardware Store and its one bin of records. My daughter bought her first CD at a huge record store with miles of aisles, but she still left the store with that same imperative to rip off the wrapper, read and reread the song list, and get home as soon as possible!

I used to get a wistful pang each time I realized that my daughter would never have that particular and peculiar plea-sure of moving a record player arm up and over, of putting the needle down, just so, at the edge of a large vinyl disk, and of hearing the slight hiss in the thin slice of time before the first song. I loved that moment of knowing exactly what was coming but still marveling at the pleasure the opening notes of a favorite album gave me every single time I heard them. I now see that she gets that same pleasure from putting the CD in its player, pushing the top down, and pressing play. There is the whirr of the CD starting to spin, that moment of anticipation, and then—bliss.

I wish I knew how the record needle turned those thin grooves into music, or how the laser turns digital bits into notes. Despite my school years as a science geek, I don't fully understand either process, but it doesn't really matter. For our kids as well as for us, music is both fun *and* essential. It clings to us and we to it. It's a reliable, pleasing constant and often a source of pure euphoria. Music can be solitary or social. It is part of the language of friendship, something just fun to have in common or a connection that makes a relationship even stronger.

I've read that of the five senses, smell is the one that most often evokes a memory of a past time or place. I have to go with sound and with song. Notes and harmonies insinuate themselves into every stage of our lives, and hearing a song can bring back great memories or, yes, bittersweet ones about an old friend or a lonely winter day.

We shouldn't live in the past, but it's okay to be a little self-indulgent every now and then. If we need to get away from some worries for a while, or just take a break from school or work, music is there. I often find that music is what I've neglected during a difficult patch in my life, and returning to a favorite album can often begin the journey back to a better frame of mind. I can just enjoy the music for itself, or I can allow the associations to flow in, whether they take me back to a certain summer, or to a college dorm room, or even to my childhood bedroom, the one with my first record player.

That bedroom looked out over just a few houses on the fringe of a small town, but it was an oasis in a larger world that mostly confused me. The world is so much bigger now, and out our kids' windows is an unimaginably vast array of rooftops and people living under them. But inside, it's still safe and familiar, a place for the restorative power of music.

worn out

W E WERE TRICKED!
For a treat on some summer evenings, my dad
took us kids to Horton's Point. A few miles of back road led
to a cliff that overlooked the immense sound that formed the
northern boundary of the string of towns out on our end of
Long Island. Way over the western horizon was Oz-like
New York City, to our east the open ocean, and across the
way, visible only on a perfectly clear day, was New England.

As we pulled into the parking lot of crushed clamshells,
all of us packed into a Rambler station wagon, a white-
washed lighthouse loomed into view. We piled out and made
for the break in the hedges at the top of the cliff, where an in-
credibly long flight of old wooden stairs descended to the
sliver of beach far below.

Having behaved like little angels at the dinner table, we
could now make as much noise as we wanted in this wild,
beautiful, and slightly dangerous place. We'd barrel down

the steps, then climb back up, counting each step out loud. We'd quarrel when we came up with a different total. Did you count the beach as one? Did the top step count? What about a broken step? Back down we'd go, and back up again, albeit a little slower each time, but we'd be sure to get back to the top in time for the countdown to the dramatic sunset over the water.

What was my dad doing this entire time? Now that I'm a dad, I know. He was also counting—counting the minutes until our bedtime so he could have a quiet evening with Mom! I'm sure he was taking in the natural beauty of the setting—and this is a particularly sublime spot that I am still drawn back to every year— but he must've also been smiling to himself that he had so easily deployed the wear-your-kids-out-by-letting-them-run-and-jump-so-they'll-go-to-sleep-earlier technique.

We all love our children, but we so need some quiet time at the end of the day—time for a cup of tea or a glass of wine, time for a book or some TV, and time to catch up on how our spouse's day went. And that's only possible with the little ones tucked away. Children resist bedtime almost as much as vitamins or hair-brushing, so in order to get the peace we crave, we have to find ways to get them to burn *all* of their daily allotment of energy.

So we take our children to playgrounds and parks, to swing and climb and run, for the fresh air, for the exercise, for the fun . . . and to wear them out. They may have been at this playground and on that slide a million times, but no matter. Down the slide, around, and back up. Down, around, up. Over and over again, never getting bored. After being told what to do and how to behave most of the day, this is *their* moment of abandon . . . *and* control.

At first we join in the play, but after the umpteenth push on a swing, our restless adult minds return to thoughts about work or a project around the house that needs doing. We see our day as finite; a child sees it as infinite.

But when we let ourselves see the world through their eyes and in simpler terms—when we too get on a swing or stack blocks or carry buckets of water back and forth from the water's edge—then we preoccupied adults become kids again, at least for a while, and *our* heads hit the pillow that night with the exhausted pleasure of a day well spent.

the size of things

GENERALLY SPEAKING, THINGS BIGGER THAN us are scary, at least at first.

For our daughter's second birthday party, my wife and I had the idea that I'd dress up as Barney the Dinosaur, her favorite TV character at the time. I rented the costume from a place downtown and hustled it into a closet the day before she was to have her friends over, or really at that age, the children of *our* friends. Before the party I told a friend what we had planned, and she warned me about bounding into a room. "You'll terrify the kids!" she said. "They've only seen a foot-tall Barney on TV, or they've held him as a plush toy."

Even after ever-so-slowly and cautiously entering the living room, "Barney" still caused two kids to run away crying. Our daughter was not so much brave as just delighted that Barney had come to *her* birthday party. All the better that he wasn't just a foot tall, but six feet tall!

I don't recall if I tried to imitate Barney's voice. (I hope not, but I do a pretty good Bert and Ernie; *that* would've added a few hours to later counseling.) Before long some annoyingly persistent boy discovered the zipper in the back of the costume. (Had I been discovered inside, it might have caused a crisis on the scale of the one when our daughter, by luck of timing, met Santa in two different malls a day apart. When the second Santa asked her for her name, she cried, "I told you yesterday!")

As a child, the things I most recall being way over my head were ocean waves. Several times each summer we'd take a break from the local bay beaches, and my dad would take us on an all-day family outing to the ocean beaches on the south shore of Long Island. We loved those trips, even with the inevitable sandy sandwiches, the too-sweet Thermos tea, and the wicked sunburns. (SPF was not a part of the lingo in the 1960s; SDS yes, but not SPF.) Even now I can recall the feeling of being terrified at the size of some of the waves. They came on as if to crash over me and my brothers, snap us in two, and tow us out. Of course, now I realize they weren't all *that* big, but from where we stood, they seemed gigantic.

I also recall that the lot next to our house seemed huge. It was the site of our neighborhood fall football games, and only the older kids could chuck the ball the length of the field.

In the summer, we played "catcher flies up," although

that syntax seems a little off. We'd just pound the baseball to each other for hours on end, and whoever caught five balls first got to be the batter. We'd repeat that cycle over and over and over again, until it got too dark to see, and even then we'd continue, breaking only to inhale dinner. Now my folks have retired to Florida and all us kids have moved away, but I've driven by the house a few times over the years. It turns out the lot where we played football and baseball isn't as big as Yankee Stadium after all.

When it was just too hot to play ball, we'd hop on our bikes for the short ride down the road to the beach. Two rafts, their blue-gray wooden slat tops looking out of our reach, floated in the calm, sheltered bay. One of our preteen rites of passage was passing a swimming test in order to be allowed out to the first raft. Later, another test got us to the second raft with the bigger kids. Once out there, we seemed to be miles from shore, especially at high tide.

The town beach was the site of many little "tests" during my teen years. One was the trek to the candy shack, a long, long walk, it seemed, all the while fully exposed to the girls, us boys with our gawky bodies and dorky bathing suits. The walk back to my towel also felt like it happened in slow motion, because I was sure that all eyes were on me and my bony chest, goofy short hair, and salt-crusted glasses. Each time it felt like the longest walk of my life.

It was only much later that I realized that *everyone* is self-conscious and dreads their turn to make "the long walk." It helps to keep that in mind. If you do, what once seemed like a daunting distance becomes much more easily crossed territory. Maybe it's just something we have to go through in order to gain experience and perspective, so we can learn what matters and what doesn't.

After all those years of foolish anxiety, I am happy to return with my daughter to some of the settings of my youthful dramas, swimming out to distant rafts or facing down those waves together. I see her eyes get big at the sight of some of those waves, but she's learned to dive in or go up and over. And I love taking that long walk with her across the beach now, her tiny hand in mine, to get some candy or ice cream.

If they look now, all they'll see is the pride in my eyes.

a single puff

I'D LIKE TO BE ABLE TO SAY THAT WHAT KEPT ME from ever smoking cigarettes was a strong will.

Yes, I suppose I was a bit of a Goody Two-shoes, a square. But I had as much of a desire to fit in as anyone. It may have just been more economics than character. Whatever money I earned went to baseball cards, comic books, and records. Cigarettes were not in my budget.

It is also true that I just wasn't part of the "cool crowd" that smoked outside school at lunch, on the way home, or while riding around in cars. It's just as well; I'm sure I would've taken a puff at the first sign of peer pressure.

So, taken together, it was lack of money + straight-as-a-slide-rule nerd + a fear of trying new things = not a smoker. Well, there was one other thing.

One afternoon I found my mother sitting in the living room, quietly savoring a cigarette. She was not ruffled that I'd found her; in fact, she seemed pleased. I said, "I didn't know you smoked."

"I don't, but I used to, back in college," she replied. "I have one a year now, just to savor the taste. Want to try?"

I took a single puff, coughed like mad, and never had the urge again.

My folks never gave me the birds-and-bees talk, their only failing in the lessons department, but they taught us so much else about how to be and what to strive for—good manners, hard work, an appreciation of all the world has to offer—and in this case, what *not* to do.

One single puff, one simple lesson.

tv money

THANK GOODNESS FOR TELEVISION.

I'm serious. For all its shortcomings as a passive activity, how can any parent get by without it? Any mother or father who says they didn't let their kids watch TV too early in life must not have showered or slept for days on end.

When our daughter was a tot, my wife would often prop her up between pillows, turn on the tube, and dash to take a quick shower. Other mornings, when our little one awoke at 6 A.M., I'd try to sleep on the couch with her sitting on my stomach watching *Sesame Street* or a video that we'd seen at least a thousand times already.

Think of the generations that learned to count with the Count. Big Bird, Elmo, Bert, and Ernie were like members of our family, and Bugs Bunny was the slightly weird cousin. *Sesame Street* broke new ground, and now there is an abundance of good educational programming. On the cartoon front, there is a lot of dreck but also an abundance of well-done, clever animation with plenty of knowing winks to the adults watching. There is a great variety of smart, well-written family-situation programs, with really good messages about making choices, telling the truth, and much more. Superb TV is still anything on PBS (except for fundraisers involving the Three Tenors or Four very old Tops), but for parents and kids to enjoy together, Lizzie McGuire rules and Bill Cosby reruns can't be beat.

There was a time, though, when we worried that our daughter was watching too much TV. Someone at work had come up with the concept of "TV money," and we adapted it to tie in with our daughter's first allowance. Each Monday she was given a cup of quarters—a dollar's worth for each year of her age. For every half hour of TV she wanted to watch, she had to pay a quarter. What was left at the end of the week, she got to keep as an allowance. For the first time she had to make a conscious decision about whether another half hour of *Rugrats* was really worth it. After all, a quarter was good for a plastic ring or a rubber spider out of one of those gumball-type machines, set in places sure to ensnare children in possession of newfound riches.

Sure enough, she started to watch less TV, read even more, *and* learn the value of saving. And in the category of unintended consequences, she honed her negotiating skills. If I would plop down next to her on the couch to read the paper but got caught watching her program, she'd ask if this half hour counted, since it was now family watching.

Ah, my future litigator. Law school is expensive; better save those quarters.

Verve
FORECAST

Lowery Music
Co., Inc,
BMI - 2:59

KF 5069
(103, 534)
Prod. by J. South
& Bill Lowery

REACH OUT OF THE DARKNESS
(Jim Post)

FRIEND AND LOVER

Production Supv.,
J. Schoenbaum

MGM RECORDS • A DIVISION OF METRO-GOLDWYN-MAYER, INC • Made in U.S.A.

directions

A s we all know too well, men just won't ask for directions when lost.

Is it macho pride, or a desire to one-up Lewis and Clark? A need to show we're in control? Does asking for directions reveal, in front of friends and family, that we are not All-Knowing and All-Seeing?

But getting lost in a car is nothing when compared to being so afraid of showing weakness as a parent that a guy won't ask for help when he's a little lost. What do we do when we just don't know the correct next step or the right response to the new situations that being a parent presents almost daily?

Am I being a jerk when I'd much rather be mowing the lawn or reading e-mails than going to yet another kid's birthday party? Do I wiggle out of some of the harder things, so that my wife has to do bedtime enforcement and dessert limit-setting? (Answers so far: maybe, and probably.) Am I just being whiny when I ask, Where did the movies, quiet vacations, and sleeping in on the weekends go? (Yes, but where did they go!?) And the biggie: Do I have the right answer for every question and situation, or do I goof and do something that all the parenting books say *not* to do? (*No,* and *usually!*)

We all arrive at any number of crossroads in life. We get there and often don't know which way to turn. Our uncertainty and anxiety can immobilize us or cause us to choose the wrong direction for a while; if it's the latter, we often realize our error and turn around and get back on track. But being a parent can sometimes feel like a trip on a long, long road, with no signs or cues from the landscape.

After our daughter entered our lives, beautiful and healthy, we were so happy, but we also saw how dramatically our lives had changed. People had warned us, but nothing prepares you for the immediate, overnight, overwhelming shift in how you do and view everything. And every day thereafter presents a bewildering array of new and confusing crossroads—if you let them be.

And I did. So I went to talk to a psychologist after work once a week for a few months, and after each visit I'd go for a quiet walk through Central Park on the way home. In just a few weeks I learned, with his guidance, that I could make being a parent complicated, or I could relax, not overthink it, just love my daughter, and the rest would follow.

A big breakthrough in our talks came when I was helped

to see that I was defining my identity by my job title, and that I had to let go of that in order to define myself as a father first. Yes, the next promotion might mean more money for my family, so I should work even harder to get it, but really, that was just a rationalization. *This* is what's rational: having a carefree weekend playing with my kid. It's more fun and healthy and sweet, *and* in the long and short run, it's more important than any promotion or meeting or memo. If I still need to rationalize it, I can tell myself that taking time away from work makes me better at my job. But that still isn't the point. We all need quantity—not just quality—time to spend with family and friends.

Another epiphany came one summer when our daughter was still in diapers and we were on a day trip out to a beach of my youth. A diaper had been changed (yes, I'd probably gotten out of doing that once again), and I was walking across the hot sand back up to the main building to dispose of the newly minted object in a garbage can. It occurred to me that I'd walked this very way many times as a kid, with coins in hand for ice cream or, later, with a Frisbee or a radio. Now I was holding a little folded-up diaper. I recall the physical act of shaking my head and wondering where "it" all had gone—my youth, my carefree days?—but wait, I was happier now! Things had changed, but for the better. How absurd and wonderful to be at peace with a package of your kid's poop in your hand.

Whenever I learn these lessons, few and far between, about what really matters, I briefly feel a sense of regret, of wishing I'd seen it all more clearly and sooner. If only I hadn't been too stubborn or prideful to ask for help before. I try and stop the "woulda, coulda, shoulda" mental detour and instead be thankful that I know a little bit more now than I did before, enough so that I can be a little wiser about the right direction to take. And the next time I get lost, I hope I will be wise enough to ask for help.

the great books versus
the great comic books

WE DO NEED OUR HEROES, DON'T WE?
When the *Spiderman* movie came out, I spared our daughter my reminiscences of how much I loved the comic book as a kid. Besides, I didn't really remember all that much about it, except for the cool outfit and Peter Parker's crush on the girl. Now there are new heroes with magical powers for her to enjoy, namely Harry Potter and friends. My daughter had avidly read all the Potter books, so she was able to compare them to these movies for herself. Thank goodness Harry has made reading cool again. It wasn't that way for me as a kid, unfortunately.

My mom was the reader in our house, and she wanted us to be readers, too. A big bookcase held volumes of the well-worn *World Book Encyclopedia,* but she also thought it'd be good to own the full Great Books library. It was such an ambitious, wonderful thought . . . and just too much pressure. I was a pretty studious kid, but even I couldn't bring myself to tackle Dante and Donne at a young age. Those Great Books were always there, in the living room, looming, beckoning, unread. There was just too much else to do: listen to records, play with friends, do homework, and, of course, read the Great Comic Books.

Along with Spiderman, there was Thor, Captain America, the Green Lantern, and the Flash. Superman was okay, but not as introspective or flawed as the Marvel heroes. To stop by Kramer's Pharmacy on the way home from school and check out the latest comic book arrivals was an important rhythm of this boy's life. So much excitement and pleasure for just thirty-five cents. (And there was *Mad* magazine, too, of course—my very first magazine subscription.) So instead of Bulfinch's Greek and Roman gods, I lived for Stan Lee's superheroes and full-color Nordic gods.

Still, my mom's influence was felt, and starting in college, I devoured the new generation of writers, from Vonnegut to Brautigan to Barth. (Would Hesse hold up now, I wonder? I suspect not.) To this day I still read a lot of fiction, from contemporary literature to the latest mysteries— anything that shows flawed people figuring out life's conundrums. Now my favorite characters don't have superpowers, just the strength to deal with life as it is lived in the real world. They don't neatly solve every mystery or climb the sides of buildings; they use the door and they make mistakes. But they do deal with life and people and situations in both ordinary and extraordinary ways, just as comic book superheroes do, minus the snappy spiderweb-in-the-wrist contraption.

As my daughter's reading matter matures, she is moving from Black Beauty and Harry Potter to the more subtle, real, and scary worlds of, well, the real world. She's being assigned some tough stuff—novels about kids in dire straits and families living in difficult periods of history. I am caught between not wanting her to lose her innocence and knowing that she will be better prepared for life by being exposed to more realistic books. I think I'll opt for a blend—the fun alternating with the complex—and let the real world come on slowly, slowly.

In a serendipitous bit of timing, the Nancy Drew classics have recently come out as audiobooks for the first time, fifty years after they became all the rage in book form. We are listening to them in the car on long drives, my wife enjoying the nostalgia of revisiting old favorites, and me wincing a little at the unreal aspects of a teenage sleuth in pearls. But all three of us are engrossed in the story about a smart girl venturing out into the world, facing danger and making logical decisions. (It is very interesting to discover how many successful women I know were once Nancy Drew fans.)

We find our heroes and role models where we can, and the great books are often the best places, as are the great comic books. Once or twice a year at an airport or a mall, I'll pick up a comic book for the hell of it. For a few minutes, it's a nostalgic escape into a world with simpler answers.

Try it sometime: put the serious stuff aside occasionally, and escape. A detective novel is a good way to do it, or a cozy English mystery, or the latest bestseller everyone is talking about—or yes, you could do worse than spend time with Spiderman or Nancy Drew.

brothers and sisters

OUR DAUGHTER IS AN ONLY CHILD.

To us, she has the best of both worlds: her own room, no sibling rivalries, and lots of friends close by. This also means she has our undivided attention, which means all of our love, but alas, also our combined watchfulness that she not be spoiled. So far so good, our friends tell us. Still, I know she sometimes wishes she had a sister. I am sorry in a way that she doesn't, as they could help each other through.

But times have changed. Our parents, like many of their generation, married young and had kids right away. My generation tended to marry later and then wait awhile before having kids. My wife and I met in our thirties and waited almost ten years before we felt we were ready to be parents. And while medical science has become much more sophisticated, childbearing is still riskier at forty years old. Every parent worries for most of the nine months about whether their child will come out okay. When our daughter arrived with ten fingers, ten toes, and everything else just so, we couldn't bear to test the fates again.

About our parents' handiwork: I am the oldest of six; my wife, the oldest of five. We remain close to some of our brothers and sisters but not to all. As the oldest, we both got the feeling we were resented for our "special status": always the first, the favored. But only last year did one of my brothers admit to me that he cringed as I took the brunt of all the parental expectations, breaking ground as the first to challenge the rules of the day.

I was envious of the brothers immediately behind me in age, as they were twins and had such a tight bond. They were identical, assigned blue or red shirts so people could tell them apart, but I knew them best, could see even the slightest differences, and wasn't fooled when they'd switch colors to foil the plan. Into my early teens I would often play with them and their friends, all three years younger than me. I could be the big kid in charge in that world, rather than the insecure one in my own age group. As I got older and more confident, I needed them less, but imagine my surprise when they grew to my height, started having new adventures around town without me, and needed me less. (It's a sobering day for an elder the first time a younger wins at basketball.) Just when we should've been there for each other more, the growing array of after-school and weekend activities meant we saw each other a lot less.

So while I sometimes feel badly that my daughter doesn't have the constant presence of a brother or a sister, they would likely follow their own paths anyway, or maybe even not get along. They might come back together years later on new terms, as my wife and I did with some of our siblings. Mostly we found we had things in common based not on being children of the same parents, but on being parents ourselves, and just people whose company we enjoy.

Over the years it turns out that each of us has three sets of family developing in sequence, overlapping and shifting in relative importance: the family we're born into, the one we create with friends, and the new one we make all on our own. Over time, hopefully, the terms *spouse, parent, sister,* and even *family* become less important than just knowing who you can talk to, share with, be with.

the most important thing

WASH YOUR HANDS EAT YOUR VEGETABLES NO dessert if you don't eat up hurry up slow down sit still sit up . . . WE LOVE YOU . . . don't touch hold my hand look both ways watch out does it hurt? . . . I'LL MAKE IT ALL BETTER . . . brush your teeth wash your face go to sleep sweet dreams time to get up get going the bus is coming . . . I'LL MISS YOU, TOO . . . how was your day? what did you learn? why is the sky blue? remember i before e . . . WE ARE SO PROUD OF YOU . . . who was mean to you? what did she say? don't let them get to you . . . JUST BE YOURSELF . . . you look fine wear that you're not wearing that be home by six be home by nine be home by midnight what's that smell? we know how that feels it hurts you'll be okay we're here for you I wish I could make you feel all better . . . WE LOVE YOU AND LIKE YOU . . . you're a great person you are so lucky we are so lucky . . . LOVE IS THE MOST IMPORTANT THING.

hey, four eyes

OUR DAUGHTER GOT HER FIRST PAIR OF GLASSES the same time I did, in third grade.

My wife and I had an emergency meeting when we got the news that our daughter was having trouble seeing the blackboard. The solution was obvious and inevitable, but how would our little girl deal with something that had been really hard for both of us as kids? For me, it was traumatic. I was already a shy kid, assiduously studious, but getting glasses was like putting a flashing neon "geek" sign on my forehead.

Maybe it's different now, what with frames of many shapes and colors—I got the standard-issue horn-rims, the ones you can buy as a gag item now. Certainly our culture has only gotten more appearance-obsessed, not less, but if crew cuts are back in, anything is possible. Still, she took it in stride. After all, her parents wear glasses and are nice people. Plus she likes being thought of as smart, which I think is just great.

Then came part two of the geek double whammy: braces. I didn't have them, but I would never have made it through if I had; I wasn't that strong. She got hers in fourth grade, which is a tad less of a peer pressure cooker than later grades, so it's good that dental science has progressed to the point that the new techniques call for intervention earlier. And how cool that she could actually change the colors of the little loops inside the braces at each visit.

So while our daughter is no less prone to worrying about outward appearances than other kids, her inner confidence shines through, and I see a kid much stronger than her daddy was at the same age.

Thanks to her, I was able to face my own bifocal purchase, another sign that my youthful years are getting harder to see, without caring what "the other kids" might think.

teachers

As our daughter moves from elementary to middle school, I hope she will hold on to the memories of her first teachers. From kindergarten to fifth grade, six public school teachers in succession—all dedicated, caring women—were instrumental in helping to form her eagerness to learn and, in many ways, her view of the world. As her graduation approached, we talked about each teacher and what she liked most about each one. She remembered best those who loved reading and science, and also those who kept the class under control so the rowdier kids wouldn't ruin things.

Her kindergarten teacher remains one of our favorites. Years ago she was the first teacher we entrusted our daughter to for the whole day, the one who had such a bright smile each morning when she greeted her charges. (And still had that smile at the end of most days!) And recently, during the fifth-grade graduation party in the schoolyard, she was the one who scooted away from her tiny new charges for a moment to give our daughter and her classmates a big embrace. There were hugs and tears for all the teachers on the last days of each school year, which was wonderful to see. I don't recall such affection for *my* elementary teachers way back when.

Sadly, most of those first teachers inevitably fade from memory, but I predict that our daughter will remember her next wave of teachers for a very long time. High school teachers enter our lives at the most dramatic time—the teen years—and their prominent place almost every day is fused with the memories of turning thirteen, sixteen, and eighteen. I remember almost all of mine, even thirty years later.

I remember so many things about them, especially some of their defining quirks. My French teacher would make the funniest purse of her lips if we got a pronunciation horribly wrong. (My best friend from then still makes that face at a "what do you mean?" moment.) Our English teacher told us that his debate teacher would throw a coin—*bang!*—into a tin can whenever someone said "uh" or "um." He didn't do that to us, but he might as well have. As for science and math, my favorite subjects, I can recall those men at the blackboard, writing numbers and symbols furiously, chalk on the sleeves of their suit jackets. I thought nothing of it then, but when my daughter's new middle school teachers lined up at orientation, I was thrilled for her as women stepped forward and introduced themselves as the science and math teachers.

Our daughter and all her friends will be pushed forward much faster now, with so much knowledge to absorb and so many new concepts to grasp. The pressure grows, too, as they sense college and career paths being set. It's going to feel at times that each and every assignment or test will determine their futures.

I hope they—and we—can keep it all in perspective. Kids, as well as adults, should approach study and tests and work with an enduring passion, with a sense that it *is* all-important, but at the moment of greatest pressure, we should all take a deep breath and remember what a sign in the lobby of her new school says: "Show up. Be on time. Do your best." The rest really will follow. We haven't asked our daughter to be a perfect student, just a conscientious one, to do her best.

I wish I could get all my teachers together in one room, so I could say thank you. I would like to give each of them a hug, or a handshake (I doubt Mr. Newton is the hugging kind), and say, "I really appreciate all you did for me." I feel I am the person I am today largely due to my high school teachers, their dedication to helping us see the joys of knowledge, and their desire to help us do our best.

what do you want to be
when you grow up?

THIS HAS TO BE THE DUMBEST QUESTION KIDS get asked.

We hated being asked it when we were kids, and yet one day, as parents, it pops out of our mouths, as if it's programmed in parental DNA. (The "career anxiety" gene resides in the strand alongside the "constant refrain" gene, the one that contains the instructions for us to place a huge emphasis on sitting up straight and eating vegetables.) Any kid who answers honestly—"Mom. Dad. How the heck should I know? I'm seven years old. Did *you* know what *you* wanted to be when *you* were seven?"—should get a pass on their least favorite veggies for a year and have double scoops of ice cream every night.

Still, what a thrill we get when our little prodigy seems to have it all figured out already. But we really do understand that this is only part of a harmless ritual. Everyone knows it's little more than a game, and no one's going to hold the other to it, but it helps us gauge what are kids are attracted to—right now—or at age five or seven or ten. It's a little window into their world or, at the very least, a starting point on what to buy them for Christmas that year. The professions of choice change every year, of course, and they should.

It is interesting, though, what that first "chosen" career is. I wanted to be a farmer. I grew up in a house on a lot developed from part of a small farm, and the rest of the field was still in use next door. Someone on a tractor came through every now and then, and he was tan and happy, just riding along. It looked like fun work, getting to play with dirt all day. I lost the desire, though, after the harvest, when the rotting brussels sprout vines stank to heaven. (Nonetheless, I love brussels sprouts now, making them the only vegetable I like *more* than the general population does.)

Of course, farming is extremely hard work, and for the rest of my years growing up, I watched the farm next door be replaced with lawns and new houses. The closest I got to farming after that was visits to roadside farm stands. All the produce looked so orderly and inviting, all set out in rows of various-size baskets. There was no hint to the many steps it took to grow, tend, and wrest those tubers, berries, and fruits from their various roots, vines, and trees in the field that stretched for miles behind the stand.

My dad tried growing a few things in our backyard, but it was always a hassle, with little to show for the effort. Some cornstalks stuck up in a corner of the yard, as inconspicuous as the hair in an old man's nose. He had an herb patch, but those little plants hardly seemed like real farming. One year pumpkin vines threatened to take over, like something from a Stephen King novel. My aunt and uncle, a few streets over, had a substantial patch of vegetables, but they had to wage a constant battle with birds and rabbits. Still, in that rural ritual of August, they'd come by some evening to proudly deliver a bag of freshly picked tomatoes.

So what did our daughter say she wanted to be when she grew up? Since she loved animals, she thought being a vet would be fine. We arranged a visit for her to a veterinary hospital, and it took about two drops of blood for her to discover that this wasn't going to be the right profession for her after all.

Every now and then we ask again, letting her know that's it fun to contemplate the options. After all, my wife and I ended up in professions that had little to do with our schooling. We were English and sociology majors who ended up in sales and marketing. I was quite the dilettante, constantly changing majors, not sure for the longest time where I might end up career-wise. I didn't know that I was being a dilettante then, if I even knew that word; I was just unable to find the thing that got me going every day. It wasn't until I got my first job in a bookstore that I found my lifelong path, and also found that to manage a business, I would need a little from each of my dabbles with various majors, from English and math to design and psychology, with a little drama and theater thrown in! Better yet, I could do this surrounded by books on *every* subject imaginable, and could touch and be touched by a poet, cook, athlete, illustrator, or novelist at different moments of every single day.

Why was I so surprised that a life in books would be my passion? From my mom's influence to my hometown library, something must've been telling me just to keep my mind open to all possibilities and that, ultimately, being a reader when I grew up was the best possible answer all along.

the wall

KIDS TODAY HAVE LESS AND LESS TIME TO DO nothing.

Not that nothing is so great—devil's playground and so forth—but we all need some free time. Because my wife and I both work, our daughter has been in school and in after-school programs from 8 A.M. to 6 P.M. since first grade. Yes, after-school is mostly comprised of fun activities, but still, a set breakfast-to-dinner schedule for kids is a fairly new phenomenon.

When I was growing up, 3:10 P.M. to dinnertime was mostly my time. There were some organized activities and clubs, but they were of my choosing. I'd sometimes walk home with a friend, and we'd play at his house for the afternoon. Often I'd stop off at the library on the way home. It was an imposing Gothic structure in the center of town, missing only a moat to complete the picture, but being from a big and noisy family, I loved the quiet rooms and the whispered requests.

In front of the library was a long granite-block wall, on which a regular crowd of guys sat like birds on a wire, smoking, laughing, and for some reason spitting, as if they were marking their territory. The appeal of the wall was its perfect position along Main Street, on the way from school to—shades of *Happy Days*—the ice cream shop, where kids with some spending money went. The wall was tall enough for these non–ice cream types to casually dangle their feet, but low enough that a coolly managed jump-and-half-turn up would land a butt firmly on top. Not that I knew that personally; I was an inside-the-library kid, not a hanging-out kid. But I saw the hops onto the wall and the nonchalant rows of legs many times, on my way in, way out, or way by.

The small library room at school was hot, bright, and noisy; the public library in town was cool, dark, and still. I can't say I worked my way through Shakespeare or Gibbon there; I recall hours spent either with *Time* magazine or a series of mysteries I devoured. I can't remember the names of the kids in the books, but they were probably Hardy Boys clones, kids whose hometowns were much more dangerous than mine, to be sure.

I still love the plasticine jacket wrapper of a library book, and the order of the place, that white Dewey decimal system rectangle on the spine telling you exactly where the book goes. (I visited a library recently and I was almost dizzy at the sight of all that knowledge perfectly lined up on rows and rows of floor-to-ceiling shelves. And magazines perfectly bound up by year! And a solicitous, patient librarian. Just sublime. If you haven't been lately, go.)

For me, the inside of the library was a little oasis between school and home, and for some kids, the wall was one, too. It strikes me now that "library time" or "wall time," from the end of school to dinnertime or dusk, can be a magical time for a kid. There might be sports to play, club activities to do, or friends to play with before dinner and homework. It is an interlude when anything is possible, when *you* get to decide what to do. In the work world, we don't get to decide. Our late-afternoon hours likely mean two more meetings or answering a hundred e-mails, but for most kids, that time is theirs to play, read, or even do homework early, so the evening is free for favorite TV shows or e-mailing friends (well, phoning friends, in my day).

In a few years my daughter will have more freedom to decide what she does with her time or, more correctly, a greater need to use any free time she has wisely as the homework demands rise. She may want to hang out on the steps in front of school, or maybe she'll have a little coffee-shop money saved up. She can talk and laugh and do nothing at all for a while. I'll be okay with that, I think . . . well, except for the smoking and spitting part, of course. And yes, I'd rather she be in the library.

home echhhhh

IT BOGGLES THE MIND TO LOOK BACK AND RECALL that boys once took shop class and girls home economics. Change came slowly to my small town and to all of America as it emerged from the 1950s, and things didn't change in the 1960s as quickly as we recall.

We would've been better-rounded kids, and later adults, had the tables—and lathes—been turned. I think all us boys would've been a lot more useful in later life had we learned to bake and sew. And girls should've been able to go home proudly bearing a key rack or a paper-towel holder made by their own hand. (I still have my simple pine bookshelf, lo these many years later, it having made the cut through dozens of moves and yard-sale cleanouts.)

I do recall other instances when the sexes were much more equal in my high school. We had girls' basketball and soccer teams, and we yelled just as hard for them as for the boys. Maybe it's because we didn't have a male-oriented football culture. My school was too small to field a team, nor could it afford the expense. Soccer was number one, way ahead of the recent boom; it was just cheaper and easier to equip and play.

Still, the memory of shop and home ec apartheid stuck in my head, so I protested when my wife wanted to buy a kitchen play set for our daughter; I wondered, why not a plastic tool bench? I was being too politically correct, of course, but I have tried to compensate in other ways; my own Title IX, if you will. I decided to not worry about the Barbies and the Little Miss Homemaker bake-by-lightbulb ovens. I've taught my girl to throw a pretty good spiral, sink five basketballs in a row, and hit a golf ball, sort of. (I'm still working on that one myself.) I just wanted to show her that she can hold her own with anyone, regardless of gender.

Even better, she's taking karate now, and though she's the slightest one in the class, the older boys know that if they ever break her heart, she'll have the ability to break their knees. Not that two wrongs make a right, but a left-right-left might.

Still, we all need to eat, and my wife is imparting the first real cooking and baking lessons to my daughter. Now I just need to convince her that Daddy is actually enjoying himself as he curses and grumbles through another home repair project.

first dance

I NEVER, EVER IMAGINED WAY BACK THEN THAT IT would come to this.

My wife and I were asked to chaperone our daughter's fifth-grade dance. *Old* people chaperone, not us! The word *chaperone* itself sounds antiquated. Oh, I'm just being dramatic; it was great.

My first big dance wasn't until seventh grade, one more sign that things are speeding up, but at least preliminary dances, then as now, still take place in the linoleumed school cafeteria. There must be some unwritten school law that says that the younger kids get the bland lunchroom, while the high schoolers get the big gym.

The most vivid memory I have of my first dance is that the lights were turned up full and there was nowhere to hide. I tried my first moves with some volatile mixture of self-consciousness and freedom. If a shy kid like me was going to find safe and familiar territory in a room with a hundred other kids, this was it. I knew this music and every beat by heart. I did my homework every night to the rhythms of the Beatles, Stones, Temptations, you name the group. Their songs of heartache sang to me: boy meets girl, boy and girl hold hands, boy loses girl, boy goes crazy without girl. A girl-friend. What a concept.

It was of little consolation to me that even John, Paul, George, and Ringo struck out with girls sometimes, too; they said so in the songs! For me to even ask a girl to the seventh-grade dance, I had to muster the courage to walk across the schoolyard at lunchtime (another one of those long walks in life), approach the object of my affections, blurt out the invitation. When I did it, amazingly, I heard a yes. (She wore glasses, too, and we sat near each other in math—her dad was the teacher—but the chance of rejection was still there.) Before she could change her mind, I turned and hastily returned to a group of boys, who I think were equally amazed at my success.

Up until this point, boys and girls had danced together only during that odd and tortuous ritual of gym class known as square dancing. (What does square dancing have to do with gym?) First came the bizarre rush of boys across the chasm of gym floor between the sexes to pair up with any of the prettier girls before they were all chosen. (Darwin must be smiling somewhere. And thanks to the mysterious Sadie Hawkins, the girls got their revenge once a year.) But after the initial anxiety and sweaty palms, we all did settle into the silly innocence of prancing around in time to a scratchy record, laughing at our mistakes, and yes, at least from my point of view, enjoying the sanctioned thrill of putting an arm around a girl's waist . . . and during school hours, no less!

To think that at one time we thought girls were yucky. Now, on the eve of the seventh-grade dance, we couldn't wait to dance with them, especially—be still our little bird-beating hearts—to a slow song. So it was that I enjoyed getting out on the cafeteria floor, going through my practiced paces, and smiling at my date. (Did we actually bow and say thank you after each song? I can't be sure, but I wouldn't be surprised if we did.)

To me, the chaperones were benign figures standing along the periphery of the room, bit players in this latest drama of my life. But I don't think our daughter saw us the same way on the night of her first dance. She would wave and smile and come over occasionally, before returning to a group of friends. Girlfriends. Boys are yucky . . . for now.

Phil~L.A. OF SOUL

Dandelion and
James Boy Music
BMI
PH-FJC 1
Time: 2:41
Arr. L. Mitchell

National Dist
Jamie / Guyden
Dist. Corp.

BOOGALOO DOWN BROADWAY
(Jesse James)
THE FANTASTIC JOHNNY C
305

my parents

M Y DAD WAS A NEW YORK CITY KID WHO EX-
celled in math and science at school but had to go to
work right after high school to help with the family finances.
He went to sea, first on post–World War II Coast Guard
duty—then to a job on a cruise ship, back when they were
few and small. He was in charge of the onboard activities and
the onshore tours of Caribbean and South American coun-
tries. (A yearly ritual in our home was his world-famous slide
shows; they were a bit long but full of anecdotes and glimpses
of distant worlds.)

So it was that he met my mom, who had been sent on a
cruise by her well-do-do parents from the suburbs. How
could she resist a tall, well-spoken young man in a uniform?
And how could he resist a cultured college kid fresh from a
cross-country driving trip with a girlfriend?

So how did they end up in our small town, far from
the city life they had enjoyed while growing up and then

while courting and marrying? (They actually *went* to the Copacabana, just like in the movies!) A branch of my dad's family lived way, way out on Long Island, a hundred miles east of New York City. Pre-expressway, this was a long, tedious three-hour car trip on two-lane roads. (Now, with the expressway running almost the length of the island, it is *still* a long, tedious three-hour car trip, now because of the waves of people going to the ocean and bay beaches. We've gone from a trail of red stoplights to stopped red taillights.)

Back then my dad would often visit his distant cousins on summer weekends. I don't know if he knew it then or if it came to him later, but he must've realized that the tip of Long Island would be a great place to raise a family. But he also would've known that doing so would put him those same three hours away from us after each of his trips. The cruise ship business was New York City–based then, and at any given time several liners would be tied up at their berths along Manhattan's West Side. After each of his two-week cruises, he would have to climb aboard the slow railcar to journey out to our town and his wife and kids. He would get a month off each summer, and he'd take us on trips to the ocean and even back to the city for the circus or the Museum of Natural History, and at Christmas, the Radio City Music Hall show, but still, he didn't get to spend enough time out there himself, this beautiful place of his choosing.

Of course, a kid's world is mostly what is within his or her immediate and selfish interest: friends, school, sports, stuff.

We didn't realize then how much our parents were sacrificing in order to give us the experience of growing up in a small town close to endless expanses of water, woods, and fields, all illuminated by what seemed like almost constant brilliant sunshine. It was the same land, water, and sunlight that would attract the wealthy and artistic to the nearby Hamptons (the light really does have a unique quality out there), but growing up, it seemed simply normal to have so much natural beauty all around.

My wife and I reversed my parents' choice, opting to raise our child in a big city. We wanted to be closer to work, so that we would not miss key events while stuck on trains and, selfishly, so that we could easily get to stores, restaurants, museums, and Broadway plays. (Lest you think we're out dining and dancing every night, for most New Yorkers just knowing these places are nearby is half the appeal.) Even playdates and playgrounds are a short walk or a cab ride away—versus piling into a car to go anywhere. It's easier, of course, that we have the one child, while my folks had six—*six!*—to house, feed, clothe, and get out the door each day.

We're also lucky that New York City is a better place to live now than it was in my father's time, especially in the last decade or two. The streets are safer, and the air is cleaner. (The smog when I first came to the city was embarrassingly bad.) The schools are good. Most subway cars and buses are clean and new, and have working air-conditioning.

It has dawned on me lately that our city neighborhood is

a microcosm of a small town. Friendly shop owners in the area know us by face, if not necessarily by name. Couples push baby carriages or are pulled along by dogs, just as on Main Street U.S.A. We live on a tree-lined street that actually forms a shaded tunnel each summer. But giving depth and dimension to this portrait of an urban small town are sidewalks and public schools filled with a cross section of America. Think of the collage that Norman Rockwell, Keith Haring, and Romare Beardon would've painted together.

We wanted a vibrant, varied, and safe place to be; my parents wanted a place more remote. Both plans required sacrifices, but both have worked out well. The best way I can think of to thank them for their unselfishness, patience, devotion, and most important, love is to do the same and give our daughter a great childhood, to fill her with love and confidence and a curiosity about the world. It's a very different time and place, yet not so different after all.

choirboy

MY DAD MADE US GO TO CHURCH ON THE Sundays he was home.

Oh, we went other times, too, and my brothers and I even sang in the choir, but when dad was home, sleeping late on Sunday was not an option. We boys actually did enjoy singing, but we also felt that every minute spent at church in uncomfortable, scratchy dress-up clothes was one less minute spent riding bikes or swimming at the beach. Before the actual church service, we attended Sunday school, where at least we got to sit casually with friends in a small group and learn about the Bible, like the part about stealing being wrong.

Alas, like most kids at some point, I stole some candy from a store in town. I can't say now why I did it. I'm sure I had the five cents in my pocket. Was it just to say I'd done it, or because of a dare from a friend? No matter. It was wrong, and it's just not something one is proud of doing. For the nickel saved on a pack of gum, I've paid how much in guilt? But gum is one thing; the stakes are higher in today's world.

My daughter will read this and say she'll never steal anything. She's a good kid, and so was I, but it's a matter of when, not if, she'll come up against a dare or an oh-why-not moment. Most likely, the temptation to steal will present itself in the modern context of the Internet and all the material that is out there for the taking, especially music and term papers. It is a certainty that sometime, somewhere, her classmates will avail themselves of something free on the Net that shouldn't be downloaded and will urge her to do the same.

I want to tell her that there will be many temptations to steal or cut corners at every turn in her life, and that I hope she does the right thing. Each time it'll pose a dilemma and require a choice, but we all need to remember that whatever we save out of our pockets for a free song or piece of candy is coming out of someone else's pocket. It is anything but free, and no matter how you rationalize it—that it's a big corporation or that everyone's doing it—it's still stealing.

revenge of the nerds

AT OUR DAUGHTER'S FIFTH-GRADE SCIENCE FAIR, she won third place for her planets and solar system project.

Like all well-meaning parents, we helped, but we tried not to do too much. She had the initial idea, and I talked it through with her to make it a more manageable project—in other words, one that would make finding the needed materials a little easier for me. We helped her get started, and she did the rest of the work.

Science and math may be in her blood; my dad and I were both good at it. My wife and daughter howled when I told them I was a "mathlete" in high school. The truth is, five or six of us boys and girls traveled the county representing our school in math contests, and we had a great time. Others may have thought we were uncool, but the joke was on them. We got to leave school early on tournament days, take a long car ride to a distant school, and get some extra credit to boot.

We also got to spend part of a summer on a local college campus in a marine biology class. We felt quite cool.

Perhaps my daughter even has the "invention gene," apparently possessed by other family members. My uncle Carl, the architect, would show up at our house each summer with our two favorite cousins and some new floating contraption strapped to the top of the station wagon. My dad's uncle Fred was a tinkerer and had a great shop in his basement; he was one of the guys who worked on the first roadside ice machine. (Okay, so it wasn't the space program.) And not to be left out, I spent more hours than I care to admit envisioning a laser lawn mower, something that would zap the grass and save me hours and hours of work on those hot summer days.

Do I think we're raising the next Curie or Einstein? No. Her third-place showing at the science fair was just great, and coming in first is not the point. We just ask that she do her best and enjoy herself at the same time.

I do still think about that unacted-upon inventive impulse of mine, my laser mower idea. The only thing standing between me and immortality is the know-how to make it a reality and transform the lives of teenagers and adults across the country. I usually think about it when I'm about to take a nap on a porch or a beach somewhere. It was a good idea, maybe a great one. I'm happy to leave it to my daughter or others to work on, to be the beaver in the *New Yorker* cartoon standing in front of the huge concrete dam: "I didn't build it, but it's based on my idea."

i'm still ashamed

I WAS VERY JEALOUS OF MY BEST FRIEND GROWING UP.
He was good-looking, well dressed, got the girls, and
dammit, he was nice and kind and smart. I was *not* any of
those things, except for the smart part; book smart, but not
life or social smart. I was so envious that at a time when he
needed my support, I wasn't there for him, and it troubles me
to this day.

One vehicle for this envy was that odd ritual of high
school life, student government elections. Intended to be a
social science lesson on the workings of democracy and government, it had the unintended effect of teaching us at an
early age that politics, like life, is about popularity first and
issues second.

And the pressing issues on the minds of us small-town
kids? Better cafeteria food! Smoking outside at lunch! More
dances! There was so much going on in the outside world
that should've concerned us more, but it all seemed so far
away, as blurry as the images on our black-and-white TVs, as

distant as the news reports coming from the small radio tucked away on a counter far from the breakfast table, and as far over the horizon as Woodstock, Selma, or Vietnam actually were.

The cumulative effect of the events shaking the country in the mid-1960s finally did get through to those of us tucked away in small towns, and late in my senior year we had a brief war protest walkout. But in our sheltered junior year, food and fun were the platforms on which we ran for the council. My best friend ran for president—and I backed the person running against him. It wasn't because I thought the other person was better; it was because I just couldn't bear to see him in the spotlight yet again.

He was hurt and confused, but to his credit, when he won, we never spoke of it. We still got together after school, were in many clubs together, and had the same circle of friends. His maturity in the matter stung all the more.

We drifted apart after graduation, crossed paths many years later, and are now best friends again. In fact, he's my only close friend from high school days. We live a continent apart, but when we do talk on the phone or see each other, we pick up right where we left off. We don't waste time apologizing for the months we let slip by; we just jump in and talk about our kids and what we're reading and who we're listening to on CD. We love each other, and I still admire him and look up to him, but no longer with jealousy. Well, maybe a little bit, but it's with a recognition that a little demon always lurks in our hearts, and that it must be ignored.

Recently, in one of our rare moments talking about our hometown—I forget how it came up—he said that he'd once sneaked up into the tiny cupola at the top of our brick colonial high school building. For a split second, I was jealous again! Once again he had done something cool, without me, and hadn't even needed to brag about it. He didn't even tell me about it until thirty years later.

By the time he did, he'd already spent a lot of time at the top, literally and figuratively. He has become a very well-respected doctor, teacher, husband of a great woman, and father to fantastic kids. But with the maturity and peace that oh-so-slowly comes with time—with the knowledge that a good person deserves good fortune—the little demon has scurried away. I have come to feel that I was by my friend's side in that cupola, and that I saw out over our little town, too, and I am happy for him and me. I am happy that this generous soul was and still is an important part of my life.

first job

WE KNOW WHAT OUR KIDS ARE DOING WHEN they're in class or at home, but what about the rest of the time?

We all try to be vigilant about the friends our kids are spending time with, but at some point we need to trust them to choose wisely when it comes to an individual or group that could influence their lives. With each passing year, though, the time draws nearer when our kids will spend a lot of time at any number of low-paying part-time jobs, to earn some spending money and even save for college. (As opposed to the jobs they will take *after* college to pay for it all!)

I had a number of pretty good part-time jobs during high school and college, and I learned about business and being responsible. Now, whenever I'm someplace where kids are working, I'm extra conscious about whether they seem happy and how the boss is treating them. After all, it's the adults our kids work with who can be very important shapers of perspective and character.

My job at our town's one and only local grocery store put me in with my first group of full-time jobholders. I could write a sitcom about the cast of characters in this place: the tiny, sweet checkout lady who wrapped each and every fingertip with tape each day like a football player before a big game; the deli manager who barbecued out behind the store every Friday in the summertime; and the produce guy with the persistent smoker's hack that you could hear throughout the store. They showed us new recruits how to zip open a carton of soup cans just right, so that the cardboard bottom would serve as a tray. More relevant skills for later life included how to trim lettuce, how to put the newer milk cartons in back, and the art of properly bagging groceries. (Yes, I am one of those guys who usually insists on bagging his own groceries. I feel this pathetic urge to tell the checkout people that, *psst,* I'm part of the fraternity, I know how, let me. I wish there was a card I could flash, and in return, I'd get a respectful nod and an "Oh, yes. I understand, sir.")

The most fun I had at the store was during the busy summer months when the town was overrun with out-of-towners: I was called upon to leave my regular tasks and go up front to bag groceries. I had a chance to behold all the pretty, tanned girls, and, of course, I'm sure they were knocked out by my short-sleeve dress shirt, clip-on tie, and apron.

The rest of the time my work involved heavy lifting, cleaning, and sweating. The adults in the storerooms did lots of swearing and telling of stories, and we kids felt cool to be a part of it, like we were being allowed into the grown-up world for a little while. You also haven't lived until you've had a chance to spend ten seconds in a walk-in freezer on a miserably hot summer day, especially after you've finished the least-favorite job: shopping-cart round-up.

The grocery job had its moments of fun, and I did learn to be on time and all that, but it was hard work. Some of my friends had jobs they dreaded going to, and later on in college I had a few lousy experiences myself. Sometimes it was just too many hours on top of schoolwork, and once it was a crazy boss. I quit as soon as I could; I couldn't afford to, but I also couldn't afford not to. Those are not the experiences I want my daughter to have.

I don't know if the job selections for teens have changed much, but it's important for kids to manage that first part-time job wisely. I can only offer a bit of advice that applies to any job or task, and even to a group of friends: find something you enjoy doing, and do it in the company of others who enjoy the work, too.

If those around you are bringing you down, move on. Again, the same holds true for friends, and sometimes a boyfriend or girlfriend. Not every situation will be perfect or ideal, and we need to give some things time, but only up to a point. When any job or relationship turns from being a positive experience to a negative one, make a change before it changes you.

WALK AWAY RENEE
(M. Brown-B. Calilli-T. Sansone)
SMASH
A DIVISION OF MERCURY RECORD CORP
S-2041
2:39
THE LEFT BANKE
Arranged by John Abbott
Produced by World United
Productions Inc.

the "good old days"

I'M REALLY NOT ALL THAT NOSTALGIC ABOUT THE "good old days."

It may sound like I protest too much, but I don't miss rotary phones, TV antennae, and weak window fans. The minute I could afford air-conditioning, I got it. Having milk and eggs delivered to our front (or back) door by a nice man in a big white van was neat, but I'll take modern supermarkets anyday, thank you. Remember when Wonder bread and iceberg lettuce were the only options in their categories? And while life without goat cheese would still be grand, it is just such a more varied, nuanced world we live in now.

Vinyl records did feel good in the hand, and I miss studying liner notes as if they were the Dead Sea Scrolls, but with CDs there's no skipping, crackling, cleaning, or turning over after side one. Books come in more formats now than ever before, and it's great to see them promoted on TV and in newspapers with newfound fervor. As for the latest gadgets, some really do make daily life easier. I'm so much more organized thanks to my Palm Pilot, especially when it comes to updating phone numbers and addresses. (This invention came along just as our friends and siblings were settling down for longer and longer times between moves. Remember how cross-outs and scrawls used to take over the margins of your old address books?)

As for the office, I don't miss life before the word processor. Remember what a big deal typewriter correcting ribbons once were? Good-bye carbon copies (cc ya). E-mail means about fifty fewer interoffice envelopes a day; untwirling that string on the back used to drive me mad. Yes, e-mail has us all on info overload, but I'll take a bunch of e-mails after lunch that I can quickly digest and dispatch over a stack of those awful, awful pink telephone slips piled on the desk blotter like unopened bills.

On the entertainment front, I like being able to rent movies that were in the theaters just last season, and not have to wait for them to show up—sometimes—years later on network TV. In the 1960s and '70s, the ABC *Sunday Night Movie* was *the* place where new movies first aired, with commercials aplenty. And the oldies were on late at night on a show called *Million Dollar Movie*. (I remember the dramatic theme music at the beginning, played as background to stunning black-and-white scenes of Manhattan, images that stay with me because they were my first romanticized glimpses of the city.)

As for the conveniences of daily life? How did my mom even raise six kids without disposable diapers, a microwave, and videos of Thomas the Tank Engine and Big Bird?! I really can't imagine.

Okay, I am nostalgic about a few things. I vividly recall the ritual of gliding into the garage on my bike, sliding right into the first slot (I was the oldest, you know) alongside the five other bikes, then dismounting and walking into the house via the kitchen door. No keys. I don't recall ever having keys in my childhood. Three-number combination locks for our bikes at school and for our gym lockers were all we needed. The only other number we had to remember was our own address, and that was only needed for contest entries involving box tops and the like. You also had to know your home phone number, of course, but that was mostly so you could call from a friend's house to ask if you could stay for dinner.

Now, we all have more numbers to memorize than coins in a bowl by the front door. We have multiple phones and phone numbers: home and work (with extensions and voice mail), plus a cell phone for each member of the family, all with codes to delete, respond to, or save messages. We mustn't forget our fax numbers, debit card pin numbers, and passwords for a myriad of computer programs and websites. Airline and hotel reservation codes read like word jumbles. Call me cranky or on overload, but I refuse to memorize the additional four numbers they've added to zip codes. And area codes are multiplying like empty hangers in a closet. I used to know all the codes for friends, family, and business customers: 202, 203, 213, 617, 914, and so on. But now all bets are off!

Not that I'm really complaining, mind you. This new world is much more complicated but also so much more interesting, colorful, and complex in the best meaning of the word. Not so long ago kids doing homework had only one encyclopedia, out of date the minute it went to press, for all their study needs, and it had to last as the source of all knowledge for at least ten years, even though history was being made every day. We can all now do a quick Internet search on any topic; the most up-to-date information on anything—from news of the world to cold remedies to song lyrics—is at our fingertips at any time of day. And if we need an array of passwords and code numbers to keep our growing bank of data and information private, it's a small price to pay.

My daughter and her friends employ a bewildering amount of coded shorthand when they "talk" via instant messaging: TTFN, LOL, BRB, and more. But it's all good fun, reminiscent of when I was a kid and my friends and I had our expressions and slang. The codes also remind me of those useful mnemonic devices: Roy G. Biv for colors of the rainbow, HOMES for the Great Lakes, and for the planets, My Very Excellent Mother . . . um, I can't remember the rest of it. Ah, they just don't make acronyms like they used to.

I'm amused, and a touch pleased, that websites have taken to adding a quaint new level of security check to one's user name and password. Many have added a drop-down menu from which you can choose your town of birth, favorite color, mother's maiden name, or street you grew up on.

I wished they'd add favorite ice cream flavor, too, but even as it's set up now, in the course of a busy day, this latest step in our technological world lets me stop and reflect just for a moment on the "good old days."

RSO

TOP LINE

STEREO
RS 8013
(RS 8013 AS)
Intl. #
2090 354
Time: 3:55
℗ 1972 CURTOM
RECORD
COMPANY, INC.

Warner-Tamerlane
Publishing
Corp.
(BMI)
From the RSO
Original Motion
Picture
Soundtrack
"SUPERFLY"
RS-1-3046
73

MANUFACTURED & MARKETED BY RSO RECORDS, INC., 8335 SUNSET BLVD., LOS ANGELES, CA 90069

SUPERFLY
(C. Mayfield)
CURTIS MAYFIELD
Produced by Curtis Mayfield

ten things that would make me a cooler dad

1. To to be able to stick two fingers in my mouth and whistle really loud.

2. To know how to perform a single magic trick.

3. To snap off a perfect cartwheel—even just once.

4. To know pi to ten decimal points.

5. To draw anything more than a stick figure.

6. To play the piano, guitar, or drums.

7. To spin a basketball on my fingertip.

8. To break a piece of wood with a single karate chop.

9. To shuffle cards with one hand.

10. To do a really good Italian or French accent.

procrastination

Well, I've put off writing this as long as possible, but here goes.

Of all the things I'd like to change about myself—and who doesn't have a list of things?—the two I most wish for are (1) to have really long, straight hair—even just for a week and (2) to lose my penchant for procrastination. "Don't do today what can be put off until tomorrow" is often my weekend motto. Of course, everybody procrastinates to some extent, and if the only alternative is to never relax and always feel like you *have* to be doing something, then I'll take procrastination any day. (For the record, naps are *not* a way of procrastinating; a napper is simply resting up in order to do more later, right?)

If I have, say, seven things to do, I often leave the hardest, least appealing one until last. After almost fifty years on this planet—and forty as a bona fide procrastinator—I'm only just learning that the yuckiest thing is the one that should be done first, because until I do it, it's always in the back of my mind, causing me worry and stealing a little pleasure from the easier, more fun things. But if you do the worst one first, you lift a great weight. Easier said than done. (How much truth is there in *those* four little words?!)

I think this is partly why I have such ambivalence about Sundays. When I was growing up, Sunday meant no school, church only sometimes, and . . . undone homework. On into college (and later with a career), I saw Saturday as fun day and Sunday as homework day, even though I often put off assignments until the evening. With each passing hour, that untouched work hung like a cloud over every Sunday for as long as I can remember.

A friend once told me that she hated the ticking sound of the *60 Minutes* stopwatch at the beginning of the program each Sunday night because it signaled the end of the weekend and served as a reminder of homework still to be done. I don't have "homework" now, but for me, the *tick-tick-tick* at 7 P.M. Sundays still brings to mind some project due at work the next day, although it also indicates that I've successfully escaped one more weekend without cleaning out some long-neglected closet!

Of course, when I finally do tackle that closet, or sort out the mountain of paint cans, or organize my sock drawer, I feel great! How absurd and wonderful is that? And *every* time I ask myself, Why didn't I do that sooner? That wasn't so bad.

So it is that I've suggested to my daughter that she do homework Saturday morning first thing, or at least put a big dent in it, and then her mind will be free the rest of the weekend. So far it seems to be working. I've started taking my own advice, finally, and I no longer dread the clock's ticking on Sunday evening.

I don't have too many regrets, but I do feel that I procrastinated away about one-seventh of my youth. But now, learning from my mistakes, I can help my daughter *and* myself get our work done *and* get the most out of our fun time. Starting *next* weekend.

saved by the theater

WE PUT ON QUITE A SHOW.

All of us in my hometown were lucky one summer to have an adult go way above and beyond the call of duty to give us a great experience we carry with us to this day. My girlfriend's mother knew that with a number of us turning seventeen and eighteen, we were going to be bored out of our minds in a small town in the summer. She knew that boredom could lead to all sorts of misdeeds, even from us "good" kids. During the school year we were all occupied with homework, after-school clubs, and sports. But those idyllic summer days of swimming and bike-riding were morphing into ones filled with summer jobs followed by nights in cars with beer. Unless she did something, we were all going to drink and drive and kill ourselves.

Despite having ten kids (ten!) of her own, she decided to play Mom to the entire town and organize a summer musical. She got permission to use an old theater building a few towns over, and then she got 150 kids to sign up to put on *The Music Man*. My best friends played the parts of Harold Hill and Mayor Shinn; my girlfriend was Marian the Librarian. Kids who normally didn't hang out together at school worked together every night at rehearsals. Her greatest coup may have been the perfect casting, right down to the bored, wayward kids of our town who were playing the bored, wayward kids of River City. I wonder to this day if that's why she picked this particular musical.

She brought in a retired local carpenter to show us how to build sets. We also made the costumes, did the makeup, and sold tickets around town. Even I was snared in this madwoman's net. I couldn't sing or act, so she made me stage manager. I told her that I was clueless about such things, but she said, "You'll be fine." I think her other intention was to make it harder for me to have the time or energy to be alone with her oldest daughter too much.

The theater was warm and musty, but we packed the house for two straight weeks that August. Many of us involved in the production went on to at least brief flings in the theater. I built sets and did lighting in college and in summer stock, but being onstage was not for me, as I confirmed during *The Music Man*. The guy who was supposed to play the anvil salesman, the one who squeals on Harold Hill, got sick the week before the show opened, and since I knew the lines from being stage manager, I was drafted.

I was terrible! Still, it didn't matter. Everyone had a great, great time, and that wonderful woman saved us all from a summer of beer bottles and no memories. At a certain age summertime can be a string of days that run together and lose their shape, but that summer there was very little trouble in River City.

cliques

Y OU PUT THREE PEOPLE IN A ROOM, AND A CLIQUE
of two will form.

Whether out of a pack mentality or some latent survival
instinct, we humans divide up into groups, consciously or not.
It's inevitable, and though the word *clique* is used pejora-
tively, it's not necessarily bad; it just is, and you deal with it.

In a small town, cliques are fluid and overlapping. We
didn't need to come together in common defense against an
overwhelming city or a huge student body. Unlike cliques in
cities and wealthy suburbs, rural cliques don't form around
money. Those are probably the most divisive ones, because
the difference between have and have-not is so manifestly
evident.

Our town had cliques of jocks, greasers, potheads (or so
it was rumored), nerds, and the student council/yearbook
bunch. Pretty standard stuff. But it wasn't all so clear-cut, as
some kids moved easily between groups.

The group I knew the least about included the guys obsessed with cars, a mix of jocks and greasers. An obsession with cars and speed is definitely a small-town stereotype that fits; some kids pass hours under a raised hood. (I had a passing wannabe phase tinkering with model cars, but I lacked the patience for all the messy gluing, painting, and waiting.) I have to say I didn't get bitten by the bug, and I looked down on the car culture, only to come to appreciate it much later. In a Jonis Agee short story, the author compares motor oil to honey, and only when I read it did I appreciate the beauty these guys must've seen in an engine. They were just as drawn to the puzzle and order of an engine as I was to, say, a math problem.

I definitely wasn't in the jock group. My cousin was the star of the baseball, basketball, and soccer teams, and I was just lucky to have him a few grades ahead of me and to be known as his cousin. He'd at least say hi occasionally, which was worth a lot of points. It didn't help me make any of the teams, but I was good enough to get by at the intramural level, and for a goof, my friend and I joined the bowling and golf teams, which turned out to be a blast. We were terrible at both, but we got to play for free and be out late some nights at tournaments many towns away. Of course, we didn't have any cheerleaders, uniforms, or a team bus; we had an old station wagon and the driver's ed teacher was stuck with "coaching" us. He'd get us to wherever we were playing and bid us adieu with "Have a good time, boys. Come get me when you're done."

There is one place where small towns come up short: watching out for those who are not in any clique—the outsiders, the loners, the ones who just don't fit in anywhere. Like runts of the litter, they are left to fend for themselves. Maybe it's changed now that teachers and counselors have been sensitized to the needs of these kids. And on the plus side of the ledger for big cities, outweighing the potential crush of urban anonymity is a generally greater understanding of individuality, even an encouragement of it.

Recently, a number of my daughter's classmates and their parents started a book discussion group, and the first pick was Jerry Spinelli's *Loser,* a novel about a boy who listened to a different drummer. We had a great discussion and generally decided that the "cool" kids who made fun of the loser were really the losers for being shallow and intolerant.

Every now and then I arrive a few minutes early at my daughter's school to take her home. I read the paper in the school lobby, but I also casually watch and listen to the kids and wonder what it's like for them now. I'm not around enough to see the cliques, but I'm sure they exist. As a parent, it's easy to spot the loners, and my heart breaks just a little . . . until, inevitably, a teacher or a counselor comes by with a word of encouragement. There is hope.

THE FRIENDS OF DISTINCTION
Arranged & conducted by Ray Cork, Jr.

RCA

MANUFACTURED BY RCA LTD. ENGLAND FROM MASTER RECORDINGS OF RADIO CORPORATION OF AMERICA (REG) MARK OWNER TMSU ® '16 MARCA(S) REGISTRADA(S)

RCA 1838
Victor

Produced by
John Florez
X2PW 9528
Timing: 2.56
℗ 1969

GRAZING IN THE GRASS
(Hou, Elston)
Anglo-Pic Music Co., Ltd.

ALL RIGHTS RESERVED. UNAUTHORISED COPYING, PUBLIC PERFORMANCE AND BROADCASTING OF THIS RECORD FORBIDDEN

the grass *is* greener

I HAD NO IDEA GRASS COULD BE SO GREEN.

As a teenager, I mowed lawns for some older folks near my house, and for the dentist on Main Street. He was busy inflicting pain all day, leaving little time to personally attack his grass. He would occasionally come out of his office on the side of his white clapboard house, a short, stocky man attired in his white coat and with his perfectly trimmed white mustache, to make sure my rows were neat and my edging precise.

He was firm yet kind and always gave me a pat on the back, literally, and a glass of lemonade on the hotter days. He got his money's worth from me. For $5, I mowed the lawn, raked up the grass clippings (no bag catchers then), and edged every edge—*every edge*—with a hand-held grass clipper.

After I had done this for a few summers, he said he'd like to reward me for my fine, fine work by taking me on a Rotary bus trip to Shea Stadium to see those lovable upstarts, the New York Mets, in a doubleheader against Willie Mays's

Giants, no less. Would I like to go to my first live baseball game? You bet! (Actually, I probably didn't say that; Dennis the Menace might say that to Mr. Wilson. I probably mumbled a shy, "That'd be great; sure.")

The big day came, and after a long bus ride we reached the stadium, filed off the bus into a parking lot full of other excited kids and adults, and made our way up the ramps to our level, as the crowd noise from inside the stadium steadily increased. My dentist/employer bought me a program, and we headed with our group to the entrance for our particular seats. As we turned from the cement hallway into the arched passage and I saw inside the stadium for the first time, I couldn't believe my eyes.

The grass was an incredible vivid green, a surreal otherworldly green. It was the greenest green I had ever seen. I just had no idea—and I was a kid who spent most of his summer afternoons pushing a mower across fields of green. I had only seen a major league baseball game on TV—our black-and-white TV. As far as I knew, baseball fields were gray. Certainly the fields we played on as kids were mostly brown from wear, tear, and dry summers.

We settled into a long wonderful day. And it *was* a great day, even though the Mets lost both games, of course. Willie may have even hit a home run, but I'm not sure. I just knew this was all a pretty special treat.

The grass was very, very green that day in the modern stadium near the still-mysterious city.

as the saying goes

"ONE THING LEADS TO ANOTHER."
We're all familiar with these mysterious but seemingly wise expressions, as they were said to us as kids, to our parents by their parents, and so on down through the ages. So much of our advice to our children is wrapped up in simple sayings like "Don't cry over spilled milk," "A bird in the hand is worth two in the bush," and "When in doubt, don't." (Wish I'd listened to *that* one more.) Many are farm related, which is hard for city kids to relate to: "Don't count your chickens before they hatch," and "Don't put all your eggs in one basket." And there's lots of apple wisdom—"An apple a day keeps the doctor away," "One bad apple doesn't spoil the whole barrel," and "The apple doesn't fall far from the tree." They're clichés, but all are well intentioned; most are worth remembering, and some hold truly useful nuggets of truth. But I've always felt there were more sides, more shades of gray, to these simplistic tidbits of timeworn, readily accepted knowledge.

For instance, it might be useful to take a moment to examine why the milk spilled in the first place, so we can avoid the same mishap in the future. Does every cloud really have a silver lining? It's doubtful, but we can appreciate it when one does. And what if you just don't *like* apples? Still, these sayings are intended to be helpful and hopeful; something to shoot for, a rule to help guide some of our ongoing decision-making.

Anyway, it's often said, by way of explanation or excuse, that "one thing leads to another." Is life really that simple, so linear and logical? And which are the occurrences that matter most, out of the thousands swirling around us at any given time? How do we know which are good and which bad?

"One thing leads to another" is often trotted out in a negative way: "Beware! A cigarette is the first step on a road to drugs—or lung cancer." We warn kids of the bad consequences of a single action, but do we do enough to point out all the good things that can unfold from a simple act? I've been lucky to have that expression mean mostly positive things. I'd also say that *many* things lead to *many* others. I think that captures the randomness and serendipity of life better, as well as our need to make many individual choices along the way.

So it was, after a string of thousands and thousands of events and choices in our lives, that my wife and I had this new life in our charge. What bits and pieces of knowledge and experience made us the people and parents we are?

What is our daughter learning from us about being a good person? And what hopes and worries brought me to this point of wanting to write it all down?

Like I said, it's many, many things. Her teen years are approaching, an exciting and difficult time, and my wife and I can help. We want her to be able to take care of herself as her world expands in scope, as will the sheer number of people in her daily life, some of whom will be good for her and some not. But more vitally important, there's so much to savor and share. This is a great time of life, and we want her to experience its joy and excitement, while having the advantage of a little extra practical wisdom.

I don't claim to be all wise; I'm learning more every day, just as she is. But as a shy and even nerdy kid, I had more to negotiate while growing up, so I made a lot of mistakes, even though I was a "good" kid. Even if I didn't deal with all the ups and downs well myself, now at least I know what they are. If I can help my daughter avoid even one mistake, if I can spare her at least some anxiety or hurt, I'll be very happy. I also want her to just have fun and to have as many good memories as possible. I don't wake up obsessing about the future (I save that for later); I just want her to have a good, fun, interesting day. The rest will take care of itself. She makes me want to be the best parent I can be, so she'll be the best person she can be. And what does *best* mean? That's going to be for her to decide, but I hope I can guide her in that direction, by setting an example (including the times when I wasn't at my best) and by observing others who can help us, just as she guides me in my parallel journey as a father.

I had a safe, fun, basic childhood. Most of it took place in a very small town a hundred miles east of New York City in distance, but light-years away in all other respects. Even though my daughter is growing up in a big city, there are parallels to our experiences. For me, it was the 1960s, a time of great social and cultural upheaval; for her, it is the early years of the new millennium, a time of great uncertainty all over the world.

For now, that's all out there, and in here, in our home and in my heart, she is my joy, and just looking at her makes me thankful to have her as a daughter. I want to hold and protect her, as all parents want to do for their kids, but I know that's not how it works. I can't be by her side twenty-four hours a day.

I do hope this pippin doesn't fall far from our family tree. Well, a little bit, but not too far. Near enough to still be under our protective covering, but out far enough to get plenty of sunlight.

So carpe diem, as the saying goes. "Seize the day." Like all sayings, it holds some truth, but there's so much that's good and important about yesterday and tomorrow.

the starving armenians

HEAR YE, HEAR YE. A PARENT IS ABOUT TO lecture.

One of the advantages of having one kid versus a bunch is that you have the ability to sit down and talk things out specifically. My wife and I were both part of large broods that, by necessity, were recipients of oft-repeated threats and cautionary tales. You know them all—the ones having to do with sharp pencils, jumping off bridges, and Santa's coal supply.

But the biggie was invoked whenever we didn't eat everything on our plates. We were reminded that people were starving around the world, and that *they* would gladly devour the peas and carrots we were shunning. My mom was fixated on the injustices in Europe, and we heard about the starving Armenians regularly. Alas, the repetition of this message and its seeming irrelevance to our lives vastly diminished its effect, which just caused Mom to repeat it more.

She was trying to do the right thing: get us to eat properly *and* teach us about the real world. I don't know how she managed five boys and a girl without packing us off to Siberia on a tramp steamer in a fit of frustration.

When it came to be my turn to issue warnings and lectures at crucial junctures in my daughter's life, I tried to not be so dire and extreme. On the matter of clothing, for instance, she has always been a little fussy about how this shirt looked or that pair of pants fit, but I took it as a good sign that she liked to look nice and neat. I bit my tongue about making an issue of the minor tantrums that occasionally grew out of this fussiness and ceded clothing matters, rightly or wrongly, to her mom.

So I was caught by surprise when, one morning before school, she had an irrational fit, an "I can't go to school looking like this" meltdown, because her jeans didn't touch the tops of her sneakers in the au courant way. So what did I, her reasonable, well-educated father, do? I played the "starving Armenian" card, of course. I didn't want to. Really. How could I have thought it was going to help, knowing how it hadn't worked on me?

Ironically, the jeans in question that day were bell-bottoms, and I had to smile inwardly at the fickle nature of fashion. Clothing flashback! In my day, we liked our bell-bottoms extra long and all the way to the ground; a really "good" pair had to be frayed in back. One day cool clothes were neat chinos, white socks, and penny loafers, and seemingly the next day you had to have long, tattered bell-bottom jeans. Then, again in a blink of an eye, baggy denim morphed into the sharp, striped bell-bottoms of the disco years. (I plead guilty as charged. Thank goodness there are no photos of me from this era.) And yes, yes, dammit, I had a brief fling with the Izod alligator, *the* shirt of the 1980s. I even read *Dress for Success* in preparation for my first big job interview. This is all by way of saying that I got that she wanted to look good, to dress like her friends.

My daughter's appearance crisis aside, I hadn't wanted to play a guilt card too early in her young life; or more correctly, when I decided to use it, I wanted it to really matter. Whether she ate her green beans or not just wasn't that crucial to me. Saying please and thank you was and is. She does her homework on time, mostly. She plays well with others. What should I really get upset about?

My daughter is a sweet kid, which made the over-the-top meltdown all the more jarring to me. To be a bit dramatic about it, it felt like we might be at one of those forks in the road where one path led to a shallow life in a materialistic, appearance-obsessed, logo land, and the other to a wider view of the world and better priorities. It felt like one of those moments when I could make a real difference and help my child understand what was really important in life and to remember that other kids in the world did not have all the things she had.

Just the day before, torrential rains had brought tragic flooding to Central America, and the pictures on the news were enough to break your heart. I told her how lucky she was, and how those kids in the floods were without a home, without food, and without clean, dry clothes. I told her she shouldn't be concerned about such unimportant things as the exact length of her jeans. She calmed down and seemed to absorb what I was saying. That evening we watched more coverage about the flood together, and we talked about what we could do to help. We took some cans of food to school the next day, and she asked her classmates to do the same. Starving people thousands of miles away were an abstraction for her, as they had been for me, but somehow I wanted her to understand that she could do something to help those less fortunate than us.

Too often it takes a tragedy to spur us to organized action, but every day we come in contact with at least one person who is needy, and there's always something we can do to help. Rightly or wrongly, I do give homeless people a quarter or a dollar, even if it is like throwing a toothpick to a drowning man, but I also have a long-shot hope that somehow those coins will add up. Everyone is someone's son or daughter, and maybe they have kids of their own somewhere, too.

I think I've found a good balance of keeping things in perspective but not letting all the bad news immobilize me. I even take a break from the newspaper some days. Sometimes you just have to let yourself look away.

Likewise, we want our kids to gather strength from the world's beauty first, and then carefully and slowly allow in the news of the day—and the lessons of history.

say a prayer

THERE ARE TWO THINGS MY WIFE AND I HAVE failed to teach our daughter: bike-riding and religion.

As to the matter of the bike, it just wasn't a necessity or even practical in the city. No room to store it in the apartment + little sidewalk room to ride on + subways, buses, and cabs to get around = no bike or bike-riding. One day on a trip to Los Angeles way back when, we rented a bike and helmet for her and held her up as she pedaled down the boardwalk near the ocean, but the lesson faded upon our return east.

I feel bad in a way, because my bike had been a ticket to fun and adventure while I was growing up. My brothers, our friends, and I would spend entire days out and about, exploring all the nooks and crannies of our seaside farming town. It was mostly flat, so our one-speed Schwinns were just fine for our needs. Helmets were not required; baseball cards flapping in the spokes were.

If our daughter were to decide to try riding a bike again,

I bet she'd learn quickly. That's been our approach to religion, too. My wife and I both went to church as kids, but we drifted away. Our daughter did read a children's Bible we bought for her, and she believes there is a God looking over us, but otherwise we have not given her any specific religious grounding. We've talked about it, and we believe she will come to it on her own at a time of her choosing.

As with the bike, I get occasional pangs of guilt, wondering if we've done the right thing. But then I realize we have passed along the most important lessons of religion: the difference between right and wrong, a sense of fairness, and compassion for others. She doesn't have an exact label to refer to a particular kind of religion as we did growing up, but she has the qualities of a religious person.

The time will come when someone will ask her what her religion is, and I don't know what she will answer. I do know that she will respect that person for the religion he or she has chosen to believe in. I just hope and pray that others will respect her beliefs even if she doesn't have an exact name to attach to them.

look both ways

AS JUST NOTED, ONE OF THE FEW DOWNSIDES OF city life involves a lack of space.

Our apartment is small; our daughter's bedroom is carved out of a former dining alcove. And we have no yard, of course, which is a shame. When my wife and I were growing up, we had only to walk out the front or back door to commence immediate, wide-open play. Oh, the city has playgrounds, but it's a big production to outfit the crew for a trek to a park. And a day's outing to the beach involves planning on a par with D-day.

So we saved up and finally had enough money for a down payment on a weekend fixer-upper, way out in a rural area an hour and a half from New York City. We would have loved to buy a getaway in my old hometown, but by then it was too expensive; it had been "discovered." That's true of any place near the ocean, as is the colossal headache of enduring traffic to and from any beach town every Friday and

Sunday. So we looked inland for—and found—a quiet place we could afford near other families and a lake; I still had to have water nearby.

While we painted and hammered, our daughter learned to enjoy the feel of grass on her bare feet, one of the true joys of life. Soon she had all the requisite scrapes and bug bites of a kid enjoying summer, plus the snowman-making experience one can't get in a city winter. We are very lucky to have this best of both worlds: a city full of diversity and activity, and the unpretentious and quieter pace of life in the country.

Of course, out near the woods, we are visitors in nature's domain. The bees and the bears are really in charge. Lightning, heavy rain, and falling trees are serious matters, as are deer dodging out in front of your car. The grass is not only greener, it demands constant attention. Hiking trails in the nearby hills require careful treading, as one step over too far can mean a hundred down. Just like in cartoons, only not funny! But mostly it's safe and fun and often idyllic.

Growing up in a small town, the only dangers I faced were injuries incurred while climbing trees (dislocated shoulder), swimming (I *hate* jellyfish), playing ball (nothing quite like a grounder bouncing up into your nose), and the occasional bike-riding scrape. The real danger came later, when kids got cars. I lost two classmates out of a class of ninety-eight kids, thanks to cars and speeding.

In the city it's hard to go fast in a car, but every time we cross a busy street on foot, we put ourselves in harm's way. An early parental mantra instructs kids to look both ways. I recall a public safety song from my childhood about not crossing in the middle of the street. (Sorry; if you're my age, that tune will be in your head the rest of the day.) But we're not even safe on crosswalks, as cars constantly try to turn and slip by right in front of you. My daughter came home one day when she was four, asking why Mommy had yelled at a cab driver and called him a "grasshole." Crossing city streets with little kids is a *major* source of anxiety and the subject of many admonitions.

Without any fanfare, New York City has recently changed many of its flashing crossing signs from the one burned into our cortexes—the "Walk/Don't Walk" combo—to a more globally friendly pair of symbols—an androgynous walking person, and an open hand that signals "Stay put." It's a nice touch, but a more serious, unaddressed issue is the growing number of delivery bike-riders on the streets, riders who fly up the avenues that go downtown and down the avenues that go uptown, paying no mind to stoplights. More than ever, we have to look both ways.

During one of our first weekends in the country, we let our daughter walk across the street by herself to go play with the neighbors' kids. As we watched from inside the front door, she stopped at the edge of the road, a road where a car wouldn't go by for hours. She very deliberately looked one way up the road, then very dramatically swiveled her entire tiny body to look the other way, then proudly crossed the street. It was the cutest damn thing.

I still don't know if she was doing that for our benefit, but we're glad she learned the lesson about looking both ways. It's actually pretty good advice in lots of situations.

city kids

IT WAS BOTH STRANGE AND EXCITING TO LIVE IN A town that for two months out of the year, others wanted to come to.

People flocked to our small, unassuming town every summer, and I guess we were flattered. It's on the quiet North Fork of Long Island, a few miles but millions of dollars from the chic Hamptons. It was once a quiet getaway for Albert Einstein, Alistair Cooke, and a few artists, bankers, and writers. (Einstein's photo still hangs in the hardware store, the owner having befriended him during the former's visit to the store in the 1940s. Mr. Rothman thought he was looking for sundials, but in his broken English, he was simply asking for sandals. True story.)

Southold is so far out into the ocean, and we were so naive about the geography of New York City that even the kids who invaded our town every summer from the city's suburbs were referred to as "city kids." It was absurd, really, and they must've thought us such hicks. But we didn't care; we were thrilled to have new friends every summer, and ones with parents who had the money to own or rent houses near the water and nicer boats than we had. The boys were worldly and cool, the girls worldly and mysterious. I'm sure they were just making the best of their fates away from their friends back home, but we seemed to fill a need in one another, and we were together every possible chance. We'd swim and sail and listen to the radio and ride bikes; it felt like it was always sunny and beautiful. It was my happiest time as a teen, a sweet spot in time, a time that wouldn't last forever, but for which we were all grateful.

These kids gave me the chance to be a different person in the summer. During the school year I was shy, quiet, "the brain," but the summer kids didn't know this. I was free of the perceptions that defined me ten months out of the year. I started to come out of my shell.

My best friend and I essentially shuttled between our school-year friends at the bay beach and the city kids at the sound beach. In retrospect, I bet the town and city girls were absolutely chilly to each other when they met at the summer dances every Saturday night, but back then I was oblivious. They certainly weren't fighting over me, but my best friend was juggling two girlfriends. I turned out to be the shoulder to cry on for his "summer girlfriend" who didn't understand why he couldn't be with her all the time. "Be with me," I longed to say. It was torture to be so close to her and have her be off-limits. I accepted my role as friend and confidant just to be near her.

As we all approached the last years of high school, summer jobs intruded on our beach time during the day and alcohol entered the picture at night, causing the group to slowly drift apart. Once some kids got cars, they got more mobile and choosy. Things were getting complicated and messy, less carefree and innocent.

Each September the city and town kids would all return to our real lives. Some of us would write letters for a while. One Saturday each winter, my best friend and I would take the three-hour train ride to Manhattan and meet up with the city kids at the fountain in front of the Plaza. We'd talk and catch up as we stamped around trying to keep warm. None of us had much money, so we'd just walk around until it was time to catch the train home.

It strikes me now that we were bored in the city on those visits, but out in our little "hick town" we had so much we could do on those halcyon summer days.

the major food group

CHOCOLATE IS A FOOD GROUP UNTO ITSELF, YES? My wife and I were both raised on a *lot* of sugar, so it's not surprising that our daughter has quite the sweet tooth. Still, we have eliminated the worst of it—the sodas and sweetened cereals—and cut down on the cupcakes.

I feel particularly strongly about soda, adulterated "fruit" juices, and flakes frosted with sugar, as I had way too much of all of them growing up. It took me the better part of my twenties to kick the sugar habit. I recall having enormous mood and energy swings in college, and thinking they were normal for kids my age. I guess I thought they were all girl- and grade-related and not the result of the globs of glucose daily injected into my system. I get so mad thinking back to my complete lack of regard for my health. One of the few conscious vows I made going into parenting was no 7UP or Sugar Pops in the house. And we've held to that vow very well.

But chocolate is another matter. It's just cruel to deprive a kid (or an adult) of an occasional (okay, daily) treat. We're good all day: we eat eggs or fruit for breakfast; for lunch, a sandwich and real apple juice for her, a salad for us; a well-rounded dinner, and . . . dessert! A magic word for our daughter, something she has come to feel entitled to, just as her cat deserves a scratch behind the ears.

To be honest, her chocolate desire is sated more often than just after dinner. There's the ice cream cone in Central Park or at the county fair, the chocolate-covered raisins at the movie matinee, and the occasional cookie at lunch. Yes, she should eat apples, bananas, and nut mix, but she's still growing up strong and lean, the dentist finds nothing to repair, and everything in moderation, I say.

Our daughter was very excited to discover one evening, while doing some homework research on the Internet, that dark chocolate contains some healthy antioxidants. Granted, that's the good stuff and not the commercial goo that passes for chocolate much of the time, but still, you haven't seen a happier kid, or father. Now if only they would find that doughnuts slow memory loss.

slow down; we move too fast

I AM OBSESSED WITH TIME, OR AT LEAST I USED to be.

While being punctual is important to me, it can become an anxiety bordering on obsession. To try and curb my preoccupation, I have tried not wearing a watch, but I just kept asking others for the time, like an ex-smoker still bumming a cigarette. I have wasted immeasurable brain time calculating whether it's faster to take one thing into a room and bring something else out, or the other way around. I could've done it five times over in the time it took to figure out which way would be faster.

I couldn't even relax with the Sunday paper. Oh, no, read faster! Another section to get to! At the age of fifty, I calculate that I've only just now read more Sunday papers than the copies I put together on weekends at my hometown pharmacy. *That* was pressure, collating all the various sections of the papers in time for the morning rush. (Just about the only

Norman Rockwellian thing I didn't do growing up was deliver papers; I don't know how I missed that small-town ritual.)

I'm hoping our daughter doesn't inherit this same time anxiety, but I'm pretty sure I got it from my dad. He was always in a rush or rushing us. Only much later did I figure out that because he wasn't home long between trips, he was trying to make every minute count.

Likewise, I'm sure my daughter notices my time anxiety, especially in the car or on a subway. I get especially annoyed at traffic or any sort of delay. She sees her mom rushing out the door for a business meeting or some other appointment. And she herself is ruled by the two major alerts that bookend a day of schedules and deadlines: "We leave for school in five minutes!" and "You have ten minutes until bed." Timeliness is good up to a point, but we all need to find some space where time doesn't matter. I have only just learned how to do this.

Recently, I arrived at a business-related dinner across town way ahead of schedule. Either I had the time wrong or the cab had wings, but I had a full hour to burn. In the past I would've been in a quandary about what to do. Scoot back to the office and do two more things? Get on the cell phone and return some calls? Scribble a to-do list for tomorrow? Thankfully and fatefully, I decided to chuck all my concerns about making the "best use of my time" and started to walk.

I've lived in New York City for twenty-five years now, but that evening I found several streets I'd never been down. I paused to look up at the tops of buildings. I observed people and how they were or were not rushing somewhere. I became a tourist in my own city. It was one of the best hours I've ever spent, and I've tried to remember that lesson and apply it at other times, too.

Whether it's five minutes or fifty in which we might have "nothing" that needs to get done, "nothing" is something. I stay off the cell phone on my way to and from work, letting some thoughts flow. On weekends, I relish a nap. Waiting for a parking spot Calvin Trillin–like, I watch people, inhabitants of a world that really could not give a damn about our minuscule concerns. Downtime helps so much with perspective, and miraculously, it often allows an epiphany—about work or people or whatever—to find its way to the surface through the muck of our overloaded brains.

When I stop and think about it, our daughter has been trying to teach me this lesson all along. When it was time for Dr. Seuss before bed, Dad's "homework" had to wait. While doing errands we can always find time to pet a dog or get an ice cream cone, which she lingers over, lick by deliberate lick.

I had never *really* stopped to watch leaves fall until we were on swings side by side when she was younger. Leaves had become, for me, things to be raked up and discarded. I had only ever looked down or straight ahead at them. But as the swing came forward and up and I relived that exhilaration of pointing two feet to the sky, my head went back and I saw some leaves begin their journey from the branch, swaying to the ground in no particular rush. It was a beautiful sight. Jeez, what else had I missed because I was always in such a rush?

So. My advice. To you. To me. To everyone.

Stop. Watch. Listen. Slow down.

Okay, let's get moving. The ice cream store closes in five minutes.

jesus christ comes to southold

IT'S ACCEPTED AS GOSPEL BY MY GRADUATING CLASS of 1971 that the second American production of *Jesus Christ Superstar* took place in my hometown.

Really. The first took place at a midwestern university, and we were next—*before* Broadway. This could be a rural legend, but I have no reason to doubt it.

Our small senior class was split into two groups for English literature. I have no recollection what my group studied (the poetry of Simon and Garfunkel, most likely), but somehow, some way, the other class studied, and then put on, *Jesus Christ Superstar.*

My best friend was in the "Jesus class." He told me that someone had brought in the British cast album one day. They fell in love with it, studied it for the language, lyrics, and drama, and then decided to produce a show! They got approval for performance rights, and in early 1971 an elaborate production by high school standards took place in our old auditorium.

The show was wonderful, magical, and electric, literally, as rock guitar dominated this new form of musical. My envy about the other group having pulled this off, with so many classmates getting accolades as singers onstage or players in the orchestra, was mitigated by the power of the music itself and by the magnitude of this event taking place in my hometown.

I should go back someday and look at the clippings from the local paper, if they still have copies more than thirty years later, and see what was said at the time. Was there controversy due to the portrayal of Scripture as rock lyric, or did it all happen so fast that the town didn't have time to react? Or was my little town more open-minded than I give it credit for?

Adding to the drama and myth is the rumor that the musical's cocreator, Andrew Lloyd Webber, came to see the show. I can still recall one of my classmates pointing to a wooden folding seat in the back row and saying, "That's where he sat."

No one has a picture or proof, but it makes an odd sort of sense that on a pretty spring night in my senior year, back when anything could happen, back before the twenty-four-hour celebrity culture, in a town not too close but not too far from New York City, this very loud event could quietly take place with Sir Andrew in attendance.

boundaries

WE LET OUR DAUGHTER WALK AROUND THE CITY with one of her best friends the other day. We didn't arrive at this decision lightly. The city is safe, but it's still a city. The rules were that they had to check in regularly by cell phone, and they had to stay within six blocks of our apartment building. Six blocks. Very clear and definable. And we gave them a time by which they had to be back. If only it was always so easy.

Probably the hardest thing parents have to do is define limits and set boundaries. Early on it's easy to know what those boundaries are, but it's hard to communicate them. Up until three years of age or so, the basic parameters have to do with eating and behaving. The tools are sweet words of encouragement on the one hand, and time out on the other. Somehow you hope your message about what's okay and what's not is getting through. For a parent, the toughest part of this phase is your children's inability to express verbally what they really need and the intensity of their emotions when they don't get what they want.

One of the best bits of parental advice ever fed to me is that the "terrible twos" are the result of children wanting to reason with you, but not yet being able to string all the necessary words together. Tantrums are just your children's extreme frustration with *your* inability to understand *them*.

The corollary of that insight is—sorry, your children do want to jerk your chain a little. It's nothing personal. Their little neurons are just firing a mile a minute, and they are eager to explore and demand, to see how far they can get. Best advice-nugget number two is that kids actually do want parents to be clear about what the boundaries are and to help them shape and understand their world. I wish I could say it gets easier for us or them, but it doesn't. It's crystal clear that spitting out food and grabbing a toy from another kid's hand is wrong. But with each passing year, the boundaries get hazier and harder to ascertain.

When I was growing up, the basic boundaries were made very clear to us, from table manners to doing homework. As for distances we were allowed to travel from home, in a world before cell phones and in a part of the world without any bad neighborhoods, it was understood that we wouldn't ride our bikes so far away that we couldn't get back in time for dinner. We were told not to go out in someone's boat past the boundaries of the bay formed by all the islands and necks of land. (The bay looks fully enclosed, but channels around this point or the curve of that island lead to open and potentially dangerous waters.)

We obey such simple rules for years, but then the teen years come roaring down the pike, and every day, it seems, there are decisions to be made about, well, everything, from choosing friends to telling the truth to smoking, drinking, and sex. You go from the simple, clear boundaries that encircle your family to a mass of overlapping and ever-changing circles of influence that emanate from new experiences we have each day, like atoms in a supercollider.

Oh, why can't the adolescent playing field be like a golf course, with white markers clearly delineating in and out? Or perhaps there's a moral equivalent to those white flags around a yard with an invisible pet fence. I'm pretty sure I'll be the first to buy a Teen GPS Device if one ever becomes available. Or better yet, a ring that glows red when a bad decision is about to be made.

Whether you are three, thirteen, or fifty-three, a lot of life is looking out at the world and deciding how much of it you want to take on. I wish I could pass along more concrete advice to my daughter, but at least we can talk about things and decide on some boundaries together.

Even when you think you have things under control, your kid will still look for a little extra slack. That six-block limit I had in mind for her city sojourn? I was thinking six *short* city blocks, up or down from our street. But, of course, she pointed out that six blocks also count in the other direction—the long blocks across the avenues. Fifth Avenue was now in bounds. She had a point; I *had* said six blocks.

Chalk one up for the kid.

ten simple rules for parents and kids

1. Tattoos are forever.

2. Burping is only funny the first time.

3. You snooze, you lose.

4. "Please" and "thank you" matter.

5. Our friends are your friends.

6. Be a kid—except at restaurants.

7. Whatever is bothering you is usually better the next morning.

8. A kiss is essential every time we meet or part.

9. You can be anything you want to be—*after* the college loans are paid off.

10. Don't worry about what others think of you—except us!

just a game

WE'D FINALLY ACCUMULATED ENOUGH FREQUENT flier mileage to go overseas as a family for the first time. The timing was just right, as our daughter would be old enough to appreciate and remember the trip, and more important, we wouldn't need to lug a stroller along!

Rome was our first destination, and we loved the people and the city's history, piazzas, cafés, all of it. Our daughter especially loved the cool marble floor of the Sistine Chapel (she lay down on it; it *was* a humid July), the lucky waters of the Trevi Fountain (and, sigh, the Dunkin' Donuts nearby), and the sheer scale of the Colosseum. (I didn't tell her that it was a scene of much carnage for the sake of sport.) Florence was next, and it was just as exciting, especially the Ponte Vecchio, the Pitti Palace, and that glorious Duomo; a lot of good food and just enough culture.

The high point of the trip was Siena. We had planned to see it and move on before the beginning of the Palio, the centuries-old horse race that takes place in the town square and is attended by huge crowds. We wanted to avoid all that madness, but our first evening there, as we walked through the gates of town, prerace celebrations were already taking place. Right in front of us a throng of singing boys and men came rumbling out of an alley, along with a bareback horse. It was an electric and serendipitous moment, and we got very caught up in the excitement of it all. Every Siena resident was wearing a brilliantly colored scarf bearing the likeness of an object from nature that symbolized his or her neighborhood. There were eleven designated neighborhoods, and eleven symbols. We bought our little one a "shell" scarf, the one those exuberant boys had been wearing. A local teenage girl showed her how to wear it off one shoulder and knot it just so. As we walked around town later that evening, we came upon townspeople in each neighborhood seated at long tables laden with food, feasting being a central part of the week-long celebration and competition that was about to begin.

It was all outwardly festive and free-spirited, but I had read in a guidebook how seriously competitive the Palio has always been—the winning neighborhood lords it over the others for the rest of the year. Its particular infamy lies in its history of behind-the-scenes bribery, cheating, and treachery. Neighborhood rivalries are deep and ingrained, with feuds going back hundreds of years. Girls and boys from different wards aren't even supposed to marry each other.

While the Palio seems exotic to us, dating back as it does to feudal times and carried out in a different language, is it really any different from what has gone on in this country since its founding? Bordering states and regions have feuds and competitions. High school, college, and pro sports teams have avid followers with deeply rooted animosities. And the Civil War still isn't forgotten in some parts of our country.

Even in the bucolic little stretch of communities near my hometown, there was a competitive tension among towns. It was mostly good fun, wearing school colors, reciting clever cheers, and root-root-rooting for your home team. It rarely turned nasty, but the need to feel that "my town is better than your town" always lurked beneath the surface. I vaguely recall an unspoken rule that you didn't date across town lines in high school! (It looks like that changed later, however, as the phone book listings from each town have taken on an amazing similarity to one another.)

So, is all this competition good? Are games and sports—and their metaphors—any preparation for real life? Sure, in limited ways, and sometimes in the wrong ways. There is too much in our culture about succeeding at all costs, especially in the business world and to the harm of so many others, as we have seen lately.

The low point comes in the form of anger generated by misplaced notions of team spirit. We Americans shake our heads at violent incidents after soccer games elsewhere in the world, but we need look no farther than next door to see parents losing their cool at Little League games.

Whether it was cards or basketball, I just never had that

drive to win at all costs. I liked to win, but I wasn't obsessed by the need to win. I want to do well, but not at someone else's expense. I like evenly matched games. There is a joy in physical activity, in moving elbows, wrists, and fingers in one fluid motion and launching a ball up and through a hoop just so, once, twice, sometimes five times in a row . . . *swish,* a lovely word for the sound the net makes. And I love it if a friend does the same . . . okay, four times in a row.

My lack of all-consuming competitive zeal will likely cause my daughter to lack that fire, too, but on balance I feel good about that. Kick a ball for the physical enjoyment of the act. Play cards as a bit of mental gymnastics and for a few laughs. Watch, play, root, and try your best, but in the end, it is *just* a game. (She has turned my sweet but still-competitive kid brother into a quivering wreck over a manic game of Spit. He used a wet paper towel to keep his fingers moist in order to get the cards out more quickly, but still he lost, as she slipped her little hand under his at every crucial moment.)

We recently cleaned out a closet and found a board game, the Game of Life. Hmmm, the game of life, eh? If only it were so easy. Roll dice, new car! Roll dice, great education!

My daughter won the first game. Okay, let's go—best two out of three!

hair

No, NOT THE MUSICAL, I PROMISE.

After a particularly stressful day at work a few years ago, I came home just exhausted. I plopped down on the couch and just stared ahead at nothing, or at the boob tube. My little one—four or five years old then— was sitting on the floor with some brushes, curlers, and dolls. She asked how my day was, and then, hearing the forlorn answer, asked if there was anything she could do to help.

She was too young to fetch a glass of wine, so I said, you know, you could brush my hair. It was spontaneous and silly . . . and wonderful.

She gathered up her things, climbed up past me, and perched on the back of the couch. She then went to work on the top of my head, brushing and parting and reparting. This just felt so good, but the pièce de résistance came with the curlers. In no time, I looked like the best customer of a Hair Today or Sheer Expressions. (You know the places.)

All my work worries melted away. What could possibly be on my mind that was more important than, well, curlers?

our own little woodstock

No, I wasn't there.

I'm pretty sure that no one from Southold went to Woodstock—the first one, that is. It was a long, long way to go, and I doubt any parents in this rural town so far from it all were going to let their kids go *there*. Like everyone else, we watched the news unfold, first of chaos and the miles of cars abandoned on the highway, and the general good spirit of the event, and then the rain. Besides, we had our nice Saturday dances, where many of the same songs would at least be attempted by a local band.

But while drugs burst into the open during Woodstock, only the first hint of them wafted through our town. A very few kids were rumored to smoke pot; you could pretty much tell by a new hair length. Most of us still had ours cut pretty short or at most a little over our ears and down our foreheads. The guys we thought smoked were very mellow and smiled a lot.

Otherwise, alcohol was still the escape of choice. Small-town drinkers are at first very friendly, then suddenly very angry. Some of the Saturday dances were getting a little out of control during the summers of the late 1960s. Out on the dunes and grasses outside the dance hall, a scuffle or two was bound to take place as an evening wore on.

I suspect that every wave of kids before us—as they were getting older and closer to legal drinking age—had their bouts with beer and stronger spirits, but with our generation it seemed to be getting worse. More relevant to me was the feeling that our little cocoon of innocent fun was starting to crack.

We started going to the dances less and to friends' houses to listen to records more. Most weekend summer nights there were lots of fine, fun parties out on warm screened-in porches or down in cool basements. We weren't always well behaved, but we mostly were, and we had warmth, food, and the company of friends.

I don't know how it started, but word spread that we were going to have our own little Woodstock. It was set to take place out behind a barn off the north road the weekend after the real event upstate. (We were always a little behind the times.) I went along, not knowing what to expect, but it was just a local band or two and a sunny afternoon, on Mr. Stepnoski's farm, not Max Yasgur's. It was all very tame; the highlight was the arrival of a couple of Hell's Angels, prob-

ably lost. We did not know what to make of this development and were a bit scared at first. The women on the back
of each bike wore only leather pants and a vest, just a vest,
unfastened. We nearly fell over. Nothing like this had been
seen in our town before.

The bikers stayed for a bit and were perfectly mellow.
They no doubt thought we were a bunch of pathetic hicks,
but we'd had our own little Woodstock and were very
pleased with ourselves. The bikers soon took off, and at the
end of the afternoon we packed up, too, and headed home to
dinner and our nice little bedrooms.

sweet

WHAT FOOD HAS AS MANY PERSONALIZED EATING styles, preparation rules, and seasonal memories as corn?

It's even one of the few vegetables my daughter likes, although braces have put a crimp in the fun of eating it for a while. I'm certain that she senses, on some primordial level, that each kernel of corn is basically just a sweet burst of sugar.

Everyone has opinions about every aspect of corn, much of it wrapped up in family traditions. One of my family's rituals called for boiling corn in a *big* pot, a pot big enough to hold a small child. We were never threatened with that fate, surprisingly, but Mom often felt the need to relate how she'd used that pot to boil our diapers when we were babies. That perked up our appetites, I'm sure. (Now I just microwave corn, the ears wrapped in wax paper. The corn stays crunchy, and there's no big pot to wash and return to what is always the scariest part of the kitchen—the pot cabinet.)

Another area of family lore relating to corn preparation and consumption involved the laying on of massive amounts of butter. As is commonly known, ears of corn boiled in big pots by distracted moms are just vehicles for butter, pepper, and salt. Corn-and-butter conjoining is facilitated by a myriad of application tools, from butter brushes to rolling trays. (I think we mostly just rolled our corn on a quickly concaved stick of butter on a dish.) Antique stores often have a shelf of corn holders—a virtual cornucopia (sorry) of cute little objects that people down through the ages have stuck into each end of an ear of corn so as not to burn their fingers. (Isn't every simple household object from our childhood now considered an antique and collectible? If only we'd known!) And last, each of us kids passionately defended our corn-eating technique: across or around.

Adults complicate corn preparation, falling into two diametrically opposed camps. I've seen good friends have words about whether the husks should be pulled back at the time of purchase or not. Okay, *I've* had words with friends about this. Even corn growers disagree, some allowing the peel-and-peek and some not. I've decided to go with the flow on this pressing issue: even corn ruined—ruined, I tell you!—by pulling back the husks too early is still good eating.

But the true pleasure of corn is watching kids with it. It brings a smile to my face to watch my daughter and her friends sit in a circle around a piece of newspaper or a paper bag and strip off the husks of a dozen ears of corn on a summer evening. As with the eating, each kid has a particular style, from manic to meticulous, and each has her own degree of exactitude when it comes to getting off every bit of corn silk.

Corn. It's all good and sweet and messy and fun, but most important, the buying, preparation, and eating of it is still all about summertime and simpler times, then and now.

polydor

BAND OF GOLD SERIES

BAND OF GOLD SERIES

Time: 2:18
Jerry Goldstein
Music-
Morris Music
(BMI)
19

MVG 520
102239
Intl. #2006 624
Produced by
Wes Farrell

COME ON DOWN TO MY BOAT
(Wes Farrell-Jerry Goldstein)
EVERY MOTHER'S SON
A Coral Rock Production

MANUFACTURED AND MARKETED BY POLYGRAM RECORDS, INC. 810 SEVENTH AVE, N.Y., N.Y. 10019

my town from a boat

WHEN MY BEST FRIEND AND I WOULD GO OUT ON the bay in his boat, all we could see from sea level were the trees and the homes closest to the water's edge. Hidden were the buildings of town, except for the top of one of the church steeples. Most of our daily landmarks were gone from sight.

A couple of creeks—or "cricks," as we pronounced it— flowed up near to the heart of town, taking several bends to get there. From land, these creeks had to be skirted by looping roads, up and around the head of each inlet, but in one case a small bridge spanned a creek right at the bay's edge. An older kid had been paralyzed due to a dive from this bridge, and every kid in town after that was told the story as a warning.

Investigating each creek, we could see some nicer homes mostly belonging to the "summer people." Across the bay the great lawns of the mansions of Shelter Island came down to the water's edge. Money gets the shoreline.

Visually, Shelter Island comes out to meet several necks of land from our side, making it look like a fully enclosed bay. But around each neck lie other islands, notably Gardiners Island, owned by one family since the 1700s, and Plum Island, mysteriously devoted solely to government research on deadly diseases. I still have the image of James Bond in *Dr. No* landing on a similarly dangerous beach. No one I knew dared to pull up a boat to Plum Island.

Just past these islands lie larger, more treacherous sounds and then the ocean. It was this combination of protected bay and open sea close by that allowed whaling ships, the century before, to seek harbor. Now the water is dotted only with small boats, the stationary fiberglass whalers of pleasure fishermen or the old boats of the lone clammers, sticking their huge rakes down to the sandy bottom and pulling up what they can. And here and there us kids in the wooden speedboats of the day zipped all around. We were either waterskiing or simply heading urgently, so it seemed then, from one place to another. Our only obstacles—besides other boats, of course—were the big sets of fishing nets strung between large posts, the buoys that marked lobster pots, and the great patches of shallow water at low tide.

We were free out there, free from having to take the same predetermined streets that we took every single day, every hill or crack in the pavement committed to memory. Out here we'd just point the boat and go. We could get some distance from everything, if we wanted: from family, school, Main Street, and all the restrictions and rules of daily life. There were obstacles and dangers, but they were generally easily seen and navigated.

At low tide, going slow and judging the distance to the bottom (no marking twain, just a not-very-eloquent "slow ... slow ... slower"), we'd try and slip over the flats. But we'd usually feel the gentle bump of the boat on sand and the gradual stop. Running aground has so many scary connotations, from the tales of whaling ships crashing near shore in a storm to our own lives, metaphorically getting stuck in a rut at difficult times.

But those summer days, in that bay, just a little way from the center of town, we'd just hop out, push ourselves free, and be on our way.

a snowball's chance in heck

NEW YORK CITY CAN BE A WINTER WONDERLAND. Snow doesn't come often, nor does it stick for long, but when it does, the city loses its hard edges and gets quiet, and I feel like a kid again. I also feel obliged to teach my daughter the joys of a well-placed snowball *splat* on a stop sign or hydrant or some other city target.

When it came to snow while I was growing up, I felt cheated. I'm not sure how or why, but the nearby ocean seemed to gobble up snowstorms before landfall. We had maybe one big blow each winter, enough to supply some brief sleighing time, enough for one big neighborhood snowball battle.

One winter a huge storm hit, and plows threw up giant walls along Main Street out at our end of town. A friend and I were being atypically naughty, chucking snowballs at passing cars from behind a snowbank. It was harmless fun, as we aimed for cars already past us, and most of the soft snowballs missed their exact mark, except for one notable instance.

The storm had been followed by mild, sunny weather. The snow was still stacked up but was melting fast. Cars made that soporific droning and hissing sound of tires on wet pavement. It was warm enough that we weren't burdened with heavy coats, which gave us that much more freedom of movement, but not movement enough, as it turned out.

It was one of those sweet spots in time, when the snowballs launched by my accomplice (whose name I'll withhold to protect the guilty) and me found their mark perfectly. But the minute mine left my hand, I wished I could bring it back. You know the feeling, the one when you want to dive into your computer after hitting the "send" key too quickly on a heated retort to some colleague. Like e-mail, the snowball couldn't be recalled. The damage was done.

We had been tossing our snowballs based on the sound of passing cars, then peering over our snow barricade to see the results of our efforts. Alas, a snowball had nailed my cousin Smitty on the back of his neck as he glided down the street in his convertible. It was that warm, and our aim was that good. And Smitty was that fast—fast enough to pull right over and to light out after us. He was, after all, the town jock, hero of all the teams. We didn't stand a chance.

Just as on those nature programs, the cougar quickly cornered the rabbit. It felt just like that, slow motion and all. But unlike the cougar, Smitty (his real name was, yes, John Smith) didn't kill us. He was, after all, family, a second cousin, part of the family branch that had been in town much longer than my family, but close enough to stop him from whupping us. My friend was covered under the friend-of-family clause, or more likely, his mom was friendly with Smitty's mom. Smitty gripped each of us tightly by the arms and gave us a lecture about the danger of what we were doing. And that he'd like us to stop. Yessir.

I like to think that he was secretly proud that one of his kin was such a good shot. As I am when my daughter lands a snowball on a tree, or even me.

teachers, part two

A T WHAT AGE DO WE START FEELING THE NEED or having the ability to think of life in terms of analogies and metaphors?

I look at my daughter, who is a pretty bright kid but not precociously so, and wonder what she makes of this complex world. I know that she keeps it pretty basic: us, friends, her cat, favorite TV programs and CDs, chocolate, sleep, and play. She is reading difficult books now, and she lives in a city, so I know she's being exposed to more and more of the nuances of life and language, that she's starting to see the layers in things.

But at what age does it really start to gather steam, this acquisition of reams of knowledge and the subsequent need to deal with the overwhelming volume of outside stimuli by using metaphor? We look to previously understood experiences to describe all the new ones. It's a wonderfully artistic defense mechanism.

Looking back, I like to think I was a perceptive kid, but I know I give myself too much credit. I describe many things about my childhood and my hometown in metaphors now, but I couldn't have done so then, could I?

I now see the necklace of small towns that works its way along the North Fork of Long Island as a string of pearls. I wouldn't have known about the famous big band song then, but I love that song now, and it's a great metaphor for my romanticized memory of the beauty of each town and its place along the single curving two-lane road.

Back then I found most of my analogies courtesy of the classroom chalkboard. I saw the ups and downs of life as sine waves, which we'd plot to represent electrical currents. I like to think that I saw my teenage mood swings as a calculable trip along a smooth course, versus that of a roller coaster. I know I wasn't so rational as to realize at the bottom of the trough that things would swing back up again. They always do, but sometimes it's hard to see up over the next wave.

Ocean waves may have been the better comparison— they are random in size and keep coming at you; you are *not* in control. I do like to think of euphoric moments in life as being like bodysurfing a wave into shore, riding it for all it is worth, or diving in and arcing back up to the surface just so.

Scientific analogies inhabited the ball games we played, whether or not we realized it. Somehow our brains calculated the exact flight of a baseball quickly enough for us to be at the proper end of the flight. We could also ascertain the flight of a snowball, this time from the launching end of the projectile. I suppose I could've thought of life as a capricious ground ball taking a wicked hop, or as a chaotic snowball fight, with lines of fire crisscrossing like mad from all angles. I have also found that Newton's principles—that any action causes an equal and opposite reaction—sometimes applies to human nature: push your brother, and he *will* push back!

I loved science and math for the singular, definitive answer they provided to every problem. In math, QED is the wonderful punctuation that signals, like a maestro's baton stroke or a guitarist's jump at the end of a dramatically long and powerful song or symphony, that—ta da!—you've solved the problem the only way it could've been solved.

And it wasn't just in math that exactness prevailed. History was taught based on the memorization of dates. You know the ones—476, 1066, 1492, and on and on and on. We were led to believe that these were exact and absolute turning points in history. And in English class spelling and grammar rules were just as rigid.

By our later high school years, we—surprise—started to rebel. "Relevance" became a major buzzword in the late 1960s. How will knowing the date of the fall of Rome or the square root of 25 help me in real life? The primer coat of ten plus years of schooling had dried, and we craved new layers of color.

Like so many things in life, *now* I get it, and I'm glad for those teachers who had the patience to—pick your metaphor—apply the primer, lay the foundation, or put up the structure on which future knowledge would be painted, built, and hung. They probably wanted to scream out, "*School* is a metaphor, you dolts! Don't you get it? This is like anything in life: first you learn the basics, and then you add on from there. Life *is* learning, and next time, you're doing it yourselves!"

Maybe they did, and I was out that day?

#*&^@$%*!

CURSING CAN FEEL SO GOOD SOMETIMES, CAN'T it? But it comes at a price.

There was a news story recently about a college football team that outlawed swearing. They had some made-up words to express some of the anger that curse words are intended to convey, but they lacked the vitriol. I've had friends who've tried to use *sugar* and other substitutes for real curse words, but I haven't managed that very well.

Okay, so I swear, though less than before. I'm trying. It's partly from an awareness that I don't have to do it to appear tough or worldly like some salty sailor, but mostly because my daughter hates it when I swear. It also costs me some money.

A few years ago she started charging my wife and me a quarter when we swore. We could hit a dollar very quickly. (My wife is no slouch with the expletives, either. Maybe all of us from big families have that knack.) It was very clever of her to levy the fine, both as a fund-raiser and as a behavior modifier. And this rule didn't apply just to us; all visitors to our home were subject to it. (One friend of ours now walks into our apartment, slaps down $5 on the hall stand, and proclaims that he's covered for the evening.)

But why do I swear in the first place? Is it a guy thing, a trying-to-be-cool thing? I've never thrown a punch in my life, but I guess swearing makes me feel like I could be a brawler if had to be. (Hey, watch the glasses.) But all it ends up doing, really, is to show one's lack of class or manners. I'm glad our daughter has been the wiser one yet again.

She does make exceptions for epithets uttered in pain, like stubbed toes (a genetic trait in our family, or a fact of life in small apartments?) and paper cuts.

Anyway, there's no fee levied on those, and that's damn nice of her!

the roots of art

I BLAME MY HOMETOWN.

I can't draw to save my life, despite having had a house full of inspiration. We had an eclectic variety of paintings on the walls, gathered by my dad from his trips overseas. My mom collected art and photography books. And best of all, we could afford the big sixty-four crayon box. Sixty-four! So what went wrong? My daughter is a pretty good sketcher, and she's growing up in the city, so I begin to see a pattern. Is it the city and its overflowing stimuli?

I recently had dinner in a large hotel room where it is rumored Buckminster Fuller once stayed, looked up at the vaulted honeycombed ceiling, and saw the inspiration for his geodesic dome. I haven't been able to match up the dates of creation to visitation yet, but it sounds plausible.

Was Fuller born with an eye for structure, or was it his home environment, as jokingly suggested by a postcard of a tomato sauce–splattered apron entitled "Jackson Pollock's mother." My mom had a stained apron! What took Andy Warhol from his department-store window designs in Pittsburgh to his famous work? I did department store displays for a while! Why am I not a famous painter or architect?

Some of the answers lie in the mountains and desert, places of dramatic contrast to almost everything we see in our daily lives. Who can ever speak of beauty without thinking of Georgia O'Keeffe and her orchids and skulls, or of Ansel Adams and his Yosemite photographs?

So back to my hometown: farmland by the sea. It could've been fodder for Winslow Homer—if the shoreline were rougher. Monet's haystacks? Sorry, just stacks of potato sacks. Desolate scenes of late-night diners worthy of Hopper? Alas, just a cozy coffee shop.

All we had was sunlight and an almost constant brilliance to the atmosphere. The east end of Long Island has a persistent light that seems to fill almost every day. Is it from the light bouncing off the water's infinite surfaces or because any interfering particles are blown away by the sea breezes? Some artists did come out to our neck of the woods, Jackson Pollock being the most famous of them. But did he paint his surroundings? No, he seemed to stay indoors and work out his inner demons on the floor.

You see, eastern Long Island isn't dramatically beautiful. Most of the clapboard homes need a coat of paint. There are waves, but they don't crash onto rocks; they just steadily move up the sand and then back out. There aren't fields of lavender, just strawberry plants. It's just all sublime and easy on the eye and quietly pretty, but it doesn't stir the artists to grand visions.

But maybe there is something elemental about a real or imagined small-town or rural setting. Most children's first drawings include a house, a family, a tree, and the sun. It's a start.

fluid states

W E LOVE THE WATER.
    Ocean, lake, or pool, it doesn't matter. My wife
and I love being near or in the water, and our daughter does,
too. She gets all graceful and happy in the water, and it's a joy
to behold. But then most kids love water, for all sorts of rea-
sons. Water means fun, friends, family trips, summer days,
and so much more.

Why else do we love water so—all humans, that is? Is it
like being back in the womb? Or is it, as my brother claims,
that the positive ions in the air near a large body of water in-
duce a sense of well-being? Or is it that wave upon wave
upon wave is hypnotizing to watch, a rhythmic, mesmeriz-
ing motion, like, of all things, fire? Water surfaces offer a
respite to the eye, which is otherwise usually occupied with
taking in the hard shapes of man-made objects. (Is there truly
no straight line in nature?)

Water just sounds good, looks good, tastes good. It's a

word that sounds like what it is. Are we just fascinated with the *shape* of water? How does it run through our hands like that? It is literally and figuratively fluid. It is magic.

It's not just the physical attributes of water that intrigue us. It implies limitless possibilities. The horizon goes on forever—what do we hit if we go straight out? Like a train track or a highway, a waterway can symbolize a path out to an exciting place, a new life. Tom Sawyer and all that. Historically, it's been said that all great cities have their knees in the water.

Just as likely, though, it may come down to our own personal sense memory, to the association of water with sun, summer, fun, and carefree days. Of course, adding to the depth of our perceptions, water presents very real dangers to go along with the joys.

We learn early on that water is ready to grab us and pull us down if we make the dreaded mistake of swimming too soon after eating. "You have to wait fifteen minutes" was the cry of our parents after we inhaled our sandy sandwiches on the blanket. I'm sure there's a Gahan Wilson cartoon somewhere of a little boy who doesn't listen to this advice, only to have his PB&J-filled tummy act as an anchor straight to the bottom.

In youth we undertake the dreaded swimming lessons— inevitably always held on the coldest day possible—and flail and strain to keep our heads above water. Once we can swim, we must deal with nature's little tricks: biting crabs and creepy plants below the surface, and on top the dreaded jellyfish invasion each August. Stings and cuts are hazards of even the quietest, prettiest day at the beach. Your food had better be fully digested if you're going to swim the gauntlet of even the most serene lake or bay.

And then there's the all-powerful ocean. Way before *The Perfect Storm,* we were all terrified by towering waves. Storms regularly batter our area, and a hurricane that locals still talk about once carved a brand-new inlet across the way. If the tides and wind are just right, the waves at the ocean beaches are huge, at least from our point of view. Worse, we risk being dragged away in the dreaded undertow, or "undertoad," as made famous in John Irving's *The World According to Garp*—a creature ready to grab your ankles and pull you out and under.

Dad would take my brothers and me out for the first few confrontations with the waves and the undertow. As we advanced judiciously into the spaces between breaking waves, timing was everything. You didn't want to be too far away to have the waves break right on you, nor too close to miss the full effect of the wave. We were looking for the sweet spot that would allow us to bodysurf safely back into shore.

Sometimes, though, we couldn't help it, and we'd be stranded in no-man's-land, with a wave twice our height headed our way. Dad would shout, "Run toward it and dive *into* it!" What mad advice was this! We didn't believe him at first, but one pounding due to hesitation, and we got it quickly enough.

Now that I'm the dad and my daughter the ocean novice, we've had our first spills and some of the thrills. We don't get to the ocean as often as I'd like, and it's a little less fun on the adult side of things, what with the traffic and the planning and the lugging of all the equipment. But once we do get there, what joy we experience, along with that little hint of danger.

The clichés abound: life is a carnival, or a bowl of cherries. I say it's like a day at the beach. There's preparation, then anticipation, bursts of activity, resting, eating, laughing, and the annoyances, and eventually it all has to come to an end. Life is also like the waves, its highs and lows: being in the trough and not being able to see ahead; being on top and seeing it all so clearly. Waves as fun and variety; waves as challenges and obstacles.

A wave approaches, and you pause, weigh risks and benefits, the chance of success, and the cost of failure. Sometimes you hang back and take the lumps; other times you charge ahead, running straight at the challenge. And often enough you decide just right and have a wonderful ride.

altered states

M Y FOLKS LOVE THEIR MARTINIS.
As kids, we weren't offered sips, of course, but occasionally Scotch was rubbed on a teething gum, a home remedy that still seems to work. Even coffee was considered an adult drink in my house.

Alcohol is a challenge that every kid must face at some point, whether in a small town or a big city. It's mysterious, dangerous, and forbidden. Mix it with boredom, peer pressure, unhappiness, or just the need to try new things, and it is a hard-to-resist force. In the 1960s in my hometown, it was also the only way to get high. We were so behind the times that pot really didn't get to us until years after everywhere else, so alcohol was the only way to alter the senses or, for some, dull them.

Little kids have a few simple—and legal—ways to get that first early rush of a mind- or perception-altering experience. You can spin around until you fall down, and you can rub your eyes till you see spots and whorls. You and your friends can get yourselves laughing so hard you lose control of all inhibitions. It's all uphill, or downhill, from there.

As I've said before, I didn't really have the means to buy beer, wine, or booze; I spent all my allowance on comics and records. And okay, I didn't like the taste much, or the feeling. I saw how other kids acted with a beer buzz, and some were sillier and some more obnoxious. I didn't want to be more of either of those things. And I surely didn't want to take anything that might cause me to let my guard down.

But that might just be 20/20 hindsight. I was mostly just too scared, and never more so than after the famous "stomach lining" incident. One summer evening a new kid in town, desperate to fit in, had way too much to drink. He was part of a large group of us in several cars headed to or from someone's house. Word later was that he got so sick, he puked up his stomach lining. I don't know if that falls into the category of rural legend, but it certainly made an impression on me. If I was worried about emotional control, I certainly didn't want to add the chance of physical pain!

So it was that my high school years passed sans alcohol. I probably would've had more fun and learned to loosen up a little bit with it, but so be it. I have certainly learned to love wine now, and I look forward to a few glasses after a long workday and especially on a weekend evening. I wonder what our daughter is thinking as she watches the adults—us and our friends—getting a little silly and loud.

There is a 100 percent chance that in the coming years, someone will offer her a beer, a joint, or something stronger. I hope that she will be afraid of getting caught, of increasing her chances of getting hurt, *and* of going down a wrong road in life. Any or all those things. I hope she'll wait until the time is of her own choosing, in a safe place, with a small circle of friends.

I will tell her that it's okay to loosen up a little, to let your guard down and laugh more, to let your mind see things in a different way. But drinking and drugs are a huge black hole, worse than the holes in outer space she's learned about in school, the ones that suck in all light and matter till nothing is left. They're like a bottomless pit. I have walked up near the edge myself—and have backed away every time.

For me, reading a perfect passage in a book, swimming in a lake, or listening to music is as much of a high. I don't expect our daughter to be a perfect kid, but I do hope she'll look for all the other moments of happiness elsewhere, to keep her mind intact—and her stomach lining where it is.

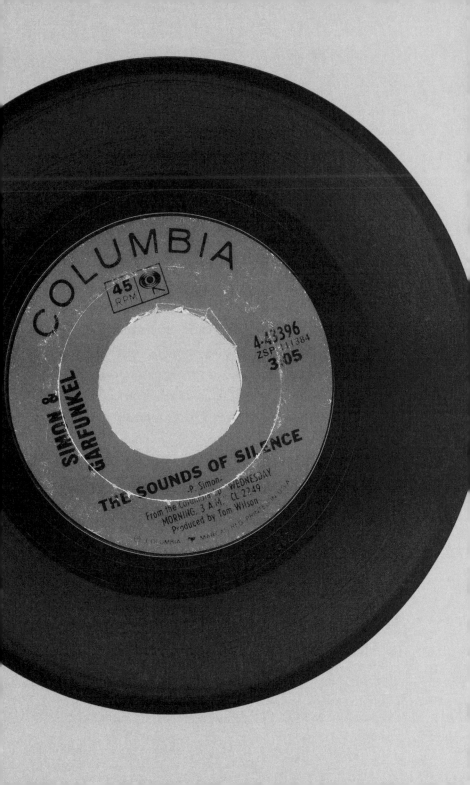

the "good old days," part two

S OME STRAINS OF WISTFULNESS WEAVE THROUGH
what I've written in these pages, but don't mistake them
for regret or longing, or a desire to go back and do it over.
Well, maybe a little.

Like fiddling with the controls on a stereo, nostalgia and
memory allow us to temporarily bring up the higher notes
and drown out the lower ones. I enjoy recalling the good, fun
things, but when I think about mistakes I made, I do feel sadness, a wish to go back and fix things, but I know I can't.

Besides, life is so good now. There's our family of three,
a few close friends, a nice home, and very satisfying work. It's
not perfect, but then nothing can be; it's damn near—I mean,
darn near. There is actually only one big thing that was better
in the "old days," something that makes me sound like the
old crank I so much don't want to be, and that is the noise
level of modern life.

I was flipping through the channels recently and came

across a re-airing of one of the 1969 World Series games between the Mets and the Baltimore Orioles. I'd seen tapes of
some of these games over the years, and yes, it's always neat
to relive that time; at the 3:10 bell we could go to the school
auditorium and watch the daytime games on a big TV set
with reliable reception. Those games and moments from
them are still vivid for me, including favorite players' unique
batting stances and the diving catches, but again, I know
that's the past and, besides, I don't want to relive the teen
anxiety that came along with, well, everything those days.

As I was about to change channels at the end of an in-
ning, a quaint little organ sound wafted through time and
space, out of the TV, straight from the stadium that distant
day. It really struck me, this antique, silly sound in the background. *That* was the one thing that was better in the "old
days": a much lower volume level to everything . . . well, until Cream and Led Zeppelin, anyway.

The barrage of noise and babble in our world today is be-
coming intolerable. TV commercials are allowed to be as
loud as the loudest point in the just-aired segment, sending
you scrambling for the volume control. Movie theater pre-
views almost blow your hair back. Some new music is more
cacophony than melody. (Okay, our parents probably said the
same thing. No, they definitely said the same thing.) Images
and noises bombard us at every turn. And instead of sweet
one-note-at-a-time organ tinklings between innings at the

ballpark, loud music is played at every opportunity, as if we can't be left unentertained for a single second.

So I vote with my actions and don't go to the major-league parks. I prefer the smaller, quieter stadiums of rural minor-league teams—cozy places that seem stuck in time—and for a couple of hours, that's okay. There's even one out in rural New Jersey now, a brand-new stadium smack in the middle of a farm field near the county fairgrounds. We've gone to a few games, and the kids enjoy the crowd, the ice cream, and the amusing games on the field between innings; only the adults get the joke that the New Jersey Cardinals' team mascot is named Claudia Cardinal.

That's enough of that rant. After all, I do love my music blasting in the car, or in my earphones while jogging. I played loud music while I did my homework in high school. I like it loud—but at the time of my choosing.

As the noise in our world ratchets up, try to remember to find some quiet in a walk, a book, a museum, or a nap. I hope we all have the occasion to say:

"Do you hear that?"

"What?"

"Nothing. Isn't it beautiful?"

geography lesson

WHERE WE'RE "FROM" IS PART OF THE DOSSIER of information we exchange at some point when we meet someone new.

Where do you work? Do you have any kids? Where do you live? And eventually, Where are you from originally? For the longest time I was embarrassed to be from a small town. That whole hick thing, or people's preconceptions of it. So when someone asked, I'd always quickly qualify my answer by adding that it was "just" a hundred miles from New York City.

But everything that was once "out" comes back in, it seems. Garrison Keillor's NPR radio program, *A Prairie Home Companion,* made small-town life interesting and multi-dimensional, if not cool, to a lot of America. A resurgence in traditional American roots music made rural parts of the South and the Midwest intriguing to a new audience. Magazines have popped up extolling the charms of country living. Maybe most helpful, *The Dukes of Hazzard* went *off* the air. Still, it took the Ice Age and a couple from California to make my hometown "cool" again.

The glacier that came down from the north stopped at Long Island and emptied out the silt of its rivers, leaving behind the ocean dunes of the South Fork. When it pulled back, it gouged out the bay, creating the forks of land. It created safe coves for the first settlers who arrived by boat, rich land for all who followed by horse and car, and great places of exploration and adventure for us kids on our bikes. (As a parting gesture, it dropped the stones it didn't grind into sand on the rocky beaches on the north side of town, creating the "ooch-ouch" beach, as we called it. We had to wear sneakers or flip-flops just to make it down to the water's edge. We locals enjoyed watching the arm-flapping, knee-jerking walk of any unprepared summer visitor.)

Things quieted down for, oh, several thousand years, until the Hargraves, a wine-making couple from California, came out to the area back in the 1980s. They saw similarities to Napa Valley, both in the soil quality (a mix of rocky and sandy; thank you, glacier) and in the buffer effect of the nearby sounds and bays. It was a true wine-growing microclimate, they decided. They planted a small vineyard, put in barrel storage, and the rest is local history. A great deal of the potato land that would've been sold off for development is now under till as vineyard. The humble, rough-skinned potato has made way for the chic, smooth grape, but it still takes the hard work of farming to bring it all to fruition.

It has changed my own town's landscape slowly and deeply; some old barns have now been replaced by very spiffy tasting rooms. The horizon is blocked from the flat road—the four-foot height of the vines on their supports is enough to keep a person from being able to see a mile over a low potato field. But I'm not complaining! It's green and productive and so much better than condos and strip malls. And there are still several turns in the main road just out of town where grapevines rippling in the wind and whitecaps out on the bay share the same vista.

I went on a vineyard tour in my hometown a few summers back and was surprised and pleased that it was conducted by the former girls' gym teacher from my days. It was interesting to hear the girls' tough-talking general—we boys used to hear her barking at her charges through the wall separating us from the girls—now talk of the careful, delicate making of this sweet nectar.

Like all kids who come from small towns and go off to college and careers feeling a bit defensive about their origins, the wines of the North Fork still have to work extra for any respect in contrast to the more famous offspring of California and the Pacific Northwest. But we're getting there, and fall traffic jams at harvest time now follow the summertime crowds. And more change is in the wind—a mixed bag: an antique store here, a new restaurant there, and some in-evitable pressure to build more houses on the water. There's a new wing on the school and the same TV channels as any-where else. The outside world is coming in at full speed now, and I hope that it won't spoil things.

When it comes my daughter's turn later in life to say where she's from, she'll be able to say she grew up in New York City, but people have stereotypical notions of that, too. I see it already sometimes. How do you live there? It's so noisy, your school is so old and crowded—where do you play?

But if someone tells her they're from a small town, she can say her dad was, too, and he loved it.

on the street where we were loved

THERE ARE HOUSES, AND THERE ARE HOMES.

In my hometown the variety of houses ran the gamut from new ranch to small cape, from old farmhouse in a poor state of upkeep to a historic white clapboard colonial eligible for a plaque. (These plaques are often found on streets bearing the names of the town's original founders, nine soaking-wet families who rowed over from New England in 1640.) My street had all the variations, and some in the extreme. Behind our two-story ranch stood a very large, two-hundred-year-old museum-quality house, while across the street stood two of the most run-down structures in town.

One of them was an old, sagging, white clapboard affair. It had a historical plaque, too, but it was not going to be attached much longer, as I knew from the few times I went inside, invited in for cold water by an older boy, Joe. During breaks in our many neighborhood football games, he would ask in all the kids. We looked up to Joe, as he was much taller, had a whiplash of a throwing arm, and called the plays in the game.

Our youthful admiration was not diminished by the holes in his living room's floor, or the fact that there wasn't a straight line in the place. Joe's sickly dad was always sitting in the same armchair, smoking, coughing, and watching a very old TV. We drank our cold water and went back out to play. Joe only showed affection to his dad, who returned it in kind. Joe was not ashamed.

As for the other run-down house across the street, we were never ever allowed to enter. I didn't know much about building materials back then, but I knew that the only thing keeping out the rain was the plastic on most of the windows and the tar paper where the shingles should've been. A little kid lived there, and his parents were rough-looking. The boy, Billy, was too wild or too young for most of our games.

Had Billy lived anywhere else in town and had we not known how run-down his house was, he would have been like most of the other kids in town. Economic status was just not a big deal. The children of farmers and doctors all had basic school clothes; logos were not a factor, and no one wanted to stand out too much. (As the late 1960s approached, the worse we looked, the better.) My brothers and my sister liked the new round of clothes at back-to-school time, but we had to make them last. We had a wonderful home, great parents, and most of what we needed. Hot dogs and beans again? Great! Corny as it sounds, we did *ooh* and *aahh* over the latest toys in the Sears catalog. I recall wanting more but being happy with what I had. We vacationed where we lived, which was fine by us. (Heck, others came to our town to vacation where we were!) We had the one car, a station wagon, but a boy in the 1960s could hitchhike without fear. I recall feeling safe, loved, and lucky.

I can still hear Billy's mom shouting out his name every evening at dinnertime, calling him home. With the emphasis on the first syllable—*BIL-ly*—this call reverberated around the neighborhood as loudly as the noonday whistle. It was quite a bellow, a daily event whose absence would have been just as loud. All we needed was one "din-ner" announced out the back door, and we were in; Billy was usually farther afield, and his mom's singsong call often went on for a while.

Now, whenever I travel back roads anywhere in this country, I feel a great sadness when I pass a run-down house. I shouldn't; it's judgmental and condescending. Kids growing up in the fanciest houses don't have the guarantee of a happy life and can often have a worse adult life, but they do have a leg up from day one, or at least the means to get help if they stumble. Kids with a lot less have a much, much longer way to go and less help along the way, but they can and do succeed if they are loved and encouraged.

Now, being a parent, I hear such love when I recall Billy's mom calling him home, and I saw it in Joe's dad's eyes when his son came in, leading a troop of admiring kids. No matter how empty or full the refrigerator or closet, there is no space limit to the love a child needs and deserves.

first romance

FINALLY, MY FIRST GIRLFRIEND.

It was the summer before my senior year of high school. It actually started at the end of junior year, with, of all things, the prom, which I had dreaded all year long. I didn't have anyone to go with, and it would cost money I didn't have. But you sort of had to go, and my best friend suggested I call a classmate with whom I was friendly. I'd never had a steady girlfriend, and time was running out. There had been one summer "romance" with a girl from the city, but that was mostly in my mind. And tons of crushes, the unrequited ones that seemingly 99 percent of all the songs on the radio were about. I was miserable.

But I called this classmate, and she said yes, and we had a nice time at the prom. She was in a large circle of kids that I was part of, a group seen by others, I suppose, as the "good" kids—the pretty studious, organization-joining, nonjock kids. The night of the prom we danced a bit (not too close), talked easily, and didn't drink. It all seemed quite uneventful, and it changed my life.

All of a sudden, I had a girl to call and talk with. Someone to take to a movie. Someone to greet me in the hallway with a big smile. And now my appearance mattered. Out with the horn-rimmed glasses and in with wire-rim aviators. The hair crept down over my ears. Out with chinos, loafers, and nerd-certified shirts; in with some wilder colors and my first bell-bottoms. (Change comes slowly to a small town. Even after seeing what the Beatles and the Stones wore, you couldn't go out and buy that style of clothes anywhere nearby, and the Sears catalog was still stuck in the 1950s.) So the time-delay aspects of our small town and my first "steady" came together that summer, and it was liberating.

The first day in senior-year homeroom that fall, the teacher went to take attendance and to greet his new and returning charges. He did a double take when he came to me. "Mr. Lennertz?" he asked, with a raised eyebrow and a slight smile at my hair and glasses. It was thrilling to finally be "cool," whatever that meant.

(As I write this now, I clearly could not care less how I look. I'm in sweatpants and an old torn T-shirt, and I'm unshaved. Later today I'll be in jeans and an old but clean T-shirt, and I might be shaved. But still, when the occasion arises and I need to wear a suit and tie, it does feel good to look sharp.)

That first romance lasted into the first few years of college, and we tried mightily to make it work over a long distance, but it's as if we had to leave town separately to grow up some more and, in the process, we grew apart.

First love is such a big part of our memory and the subject of so many books and movies and music. It's one of the most amazing, confusing, heartbreaking, and exhilarating experiences anyone can have. I want my daughter to feel the joy of it, but I dread the rest of it for her. My wife and I will be full of advice, but will she listen?

One of the most naive aspects of first love is that you think it will last forever: this is it, and nothing can change it. You do *not* want to hear from anyone to be careful and to not get your heart broken. It's you two, and you know better, and you love each other and every song you hear only reaffirms that this is right and good and strong.

In a few years (no rush!) our daughter will bring her first date home to meet us. She may fall in love and feel that absolute joy; I hope she does. And her mom and I will try really, really, really hard not to say, "Oh you're so young," even though we'll be thinking it. All we have done has been to love her, to give her strength, self-confidence, and wisdom, and then hope that when the time comes, she'll find someone who will love and respect her, never hurt her, and be the one for a summer, for a few years, or even forever.

I'm calm about this now, but I'm going to be a wreck when the time comes. I hope my daughter is patient with me, that *she* tells *me* to be strong and wise and secure. And to be happy for her.

like father, like son

L IKE MOST KIDS, I DIDN'T THINK MY FATHER WAS very cool.

In fact, I didn't like him very much during my teen years. My normal teenage rebellion was magnified tenfold by the extreme pull of the 1960s, and we just disagreed about, well, everything.

So imagine my surprise now that I've turned out to be like him in many ways. Certainly not in all ways, especially when it comes to politics. (He hated Democrats so much that he never stopped calling it Idlewild Airport.) But I'm like him in enough ways that I have to wonder if there's more to genetics than big ears and broad shoulders. Or does it just take time and experience to accept that a basic set of principles has stood the test of time and that we all come to adopt them eventually, especially when it comes to raising our own kids?

Now I see the balancing act that is being a parent, and

how much is selfish (our own need to be seen as good parents) and unselfish (our need to raise happy, healthy kids). I see that my long hair represented to my dad the chance that I was going down a wrong road, or worse—for a Depression-era kid like my dad—that I'd never get a good job looking like *that*. He really did want me to be happy and have a good life, but he also saw it as a failure on his part if I didn't succeed in all the accepted ways of his time.

Looking back, I see my dad's balancing act, the fun as well as the strict. He was always on us to sit up straight, do the chores, and so on, but he was also the organizer of game nights and the leader of excursions to the ocean or the city. At the beach he was the human diving platform. We would clamor to be the next to jump off his shoulders or be thrown backward into the air from his two-handed launching pad. And his work was never done; after a long drive back from a family trip to the city, he had to carry all of us sleeping kids into the house.

I thought I had become an adult when I got my first apartment and paid my first utility bill; then when I got my first job that required a suit; and then when I got married and bought a house. But now I never feel more adult—more responsible, at peace, vulnerable, fulfilled, and full of love and in need of love—than when my daughter jumps off my shoulders into the water, or when I carry her upstairs to bed after a late-night car ride back from somewhere.

As I reach for her in the car, as her arms instinctively cling around my neck, and as my hands lock together to support her weight, I wish she'd never grow up and never stop needing us. But knowing that she too may rebel and move away, I just hope we've given her, as our folks did for us, the unqualified love that is the key ingredient for any child to become an adult, on her own terms and in her own due time.

cursed by a happy childhood:
a time and a place for everything

MY CHILDHOOD BEDROOM WINDOW LOOKED OUT over a typical rural backyard, complete with clothes-line, birdbath, some garden beds, a picnic table, and a tower-ing black walnut tree. To the right was a small farm, separated from our yard by a tall hedge. In the plot behind our house stood a huge shingled colonial house built in the late 1700s. This town of mine was founded in 1640, and many houses carried a plaque with a date that was so distant in the past, it seemed unreal to us. Our house was a new one, a two-story ranch. We were newcomers in a place where some families went back dozens of generations. Street signs, and pages filled with similar last names in the small phone book, stood as testimony to the original families who came over from England.

Our house was just off Main Street as it headed out of town toward the next town. Our side street marked the end of the downtown businesses. An empty gas station, a place of many adventures, stood on the corner. I can, all these years later, mentally ride my bike from our driveway toward town and school, visualizing every house and storefront on each side of the street and every buckle and gap in the sidewalk. My own personal movie camera of a brain has the final edited version stored safely in my head. It took hundreds of takes and retakes, looking ahead, side to side, and down, as I navigated curbs and lifts in the sidewalk. Each square of concrete is a frame in my little drama of going to school or setting off for the beach.

When we think of a small town, we most likely conjure up a pair of stereotypical images. There's the picture-postcard one, with a church and steeple, a few shops, beautiful old homes, and tree-lined streets. The other is the noir-movie one, with ramshackle buildings, a single traffic light, and not much else. Southold, New York, my hometown, was—and still is—an amalgam of those two extremes, with enough nuance to make it mysterious and enough sameness to maintain a plain, modest beauty.

As you came in from the string of towns to the west, the first business you encountered was a marina, with boats of all sizes out front, any one of which we would've loved to own, and an inlet to the bay out back. This was the first reminder, after a long stretch of farmland, that all these towns are actually surrounded by water. More landmarks, in this order: a funeral home (often one of the nicest houses in any town;

why is that?), an Elks hall (what goes on in there?), and then a dramatic, swooping bend in the road, with a flashing light and big caution signs. We grew up hearing tales of tragic accidents at this turn; we had our own dead man's curve, right there at the entrance to town.

Coming out of the curve, a huge white stucco Roman Catholic church stood on the left, and a little farther on, on the right, a white clapboard Presbyterian church, along with a cemetery surrounded by an immaculate white picket fence. It would've been more orderly, as it was in the nearby towns, for our wide, three-story-tall, brick colonial school building to come next, but it stood down a side street between the churches.

Next came a car dealership and the requisite string of plastic flags that caught any breeze, some homes, a creepy abandoned lot (still abandoned and still creepy, despite some new buildings nearby), a Gothic library building, a small post office, and a several-block-long stretch of businesses, all in simple one- or two-story buildings, except for the bank, of course. The bank, even in this small town, was a grand, substantial affair, standing haughtily across from the only gas station and the only supermarket at the, yes, only stoplight in town. Moving past the heart of town, there was the volunteer firehouse—also home to the fair and amusement rides each Fourth of July, a big big deal in a small town—and a number of very old historic homes of either white or gray shingle. All in all, it was a safe, manageable, knowable center of town, especially for a kid.

Small-town life requires an economical act of greeting others on the street, one with an air of modesty and simplicity. We develop our own greeting style over time; it's as unique as a fingerprint. But we begin with our town's basic style. In a small town with a New England heritage like the one I grew up in, as austere a greeting as possible was desired. If you were riding your bike and you passed an acquaintance, you'd lift your right index finger off your handlebars. Nothing more, nothing less. Same if you were driving a car. In school hallways, the frequency of passing was such that the finger lift wasn't required; you'd wear it out. But I recall saying "Hey" a lot, with a slight upward movement of the head. But that was it. (The puritanical origins of the town ruled the halls, too, as PDAs—public displays of affection—were forbidden. Even the most chaste hand-holding was not allowed.)

Traveling the roads of my hometown now, I don't recognize anyone, of course, which is okay, as it gives me time to observe the surroundings more closely. Many buildings have received a new coat of paint in the more than thirty years since I left town, and the whole area is now designated a National Historic District, but the essence of the place hasn't changed. Not the nearby natural beauty and landscape, not my memory of it. On a recent visit, it was all very familiar and beautiful.

North of Main Street the houses space out quickly and the farms stretch on a mile or so, ending in a wall of trees. This band of woods backs up to marshes, batches of summer homes, and the Long Island Sound. At regular intervals the shoreline rises up to dramatic cliffs that dot the entire length of the north shore of the 120-mile-long, fish-shaped island that extends from New York City out into the Atlantic Ocean.

If the fish's head starts at the city, a hundred miles out the body splits into two fins. My town sits on the shorter, quieter fin known as the North Fork, pointing up toward New England across the oceanlike sound; the South Fork, home to the Hamptons, got the real ocean and most of the people, which was fine by us.

Since the string of towns along the North Fork grew up at the heads of the many harbors created by the bay that lies between the forks, the main road plays connect-the-dots with the shoreline. North of the main road is that flat, open run of land to the sound; to the south, it's a jigsaw of oddly shaped spits of land, all with names linked to the past: Nassau Point, Jockey Creek, Founder's Landing. This unique geography and all that lovely sand and soil made life here bountiful. Combine that with our proximity to New York and New England and you have some very interesting history. The Indians hunted in the woods, grew a variety of crops, and fished wherever salt water met fresh. There were twelve distinct tribes on Long Island at one time, most sharing the

Algonquian language. Their mark is still on the area, with
Indian place-names vying with English ones for space on the
map. The fruit that is most protected by the ameliorating effect of Peconic (Indian for "a place of many streams") Bay is
the grape, and many of the new vineyards pay homage in
their appellations to the true first settlers. (One of the tribes
closer in to the city was named the Canarsie, and I can't help
but think they were an especially tough tribe.)

The waters of Long Island also have historical, military,
and commercial significance. There was the Revolutionary
War occupation by the British, a few naval engagements in
1812, and rumored sightings of U-boats offshore in the 1940s.
And while the area was hardly the Barbary Coast, two
nearby towns were thriving whaling ports and then entry
points for rum bound for New York City during Prohibition.
And yes, Captain Kidd buried some gold on Gardiners
Island out in the bay. (Memo: It's gone now.) Things are
much tamer now; charter fishing boats stocked with beer
rule the waves on weekends.

Back on land, the area did not become so organized and
overwhelmingly agricultural until a wave of Polish farmers
arrived in the late 1800s. Everyone and everything seemed to
thrive here, and we have the roadside stands, festivals (along
with a Strawberry Queen), and pies to prove it. And the corn,
the corn; don't get me started again.

There are a number of roadside historical markers
around town noting famous battles or original settlements,

but there are no signs announcing my three favorite bits of local history: the first silent movies were filmed on the dunes of the Hamptons, Walt Whitman was a bit of a local character, and Albert Einstein's letter to FDR about the bomb was postmarked from the next town over from mine.

Paradoxes abound in many towns, but my town at that time was a particularly peculiar and special place. Looking back now, I can see that its size, geography, and place on the map allowed the changing world to seep in gradually, giving us kids in the 1960s time to digest and adjust in a place far but not too far from New York City. And where else could soil and sea, open fields and hidden coves, tractors and fishing boats so closely coexist? From a few spots, locals and visitors alike could look one way and see old barns and cornstalks, then turn the other way and see boats and white-capped waves, and know that both vistas could have been unchanged for hundreds of years. But they were changing, slowly, and mostly for the good.

The distance from the city was being bridged by the speedier transmission of both exciting and troubling news from the rest of the world. New television shows, images of war and strife, rock and roll at more stops of the dial, brighter clothes in the stores, and provocative new books and magazines were now coming in more clearly, loudly, and frequently.

Yes, we sensed big change was coming, with the outside world turning upside down along with our hormones. But the serene views out our bedroom and car windows said everything was the same. In most every direction we kids looked and listened, we still saw, heard, and anticipated just another day of fun. We were naive, protected—and just beginning to get a little restless.

I am lucky to have this had this almost idyllic childhood, luckier still to have the memories preserved untouched. My dad waited for me to graduate from high school before moving the family to the Boston area for a new job. In quick succession came my eighteenth birthday, college, and new friends. I had no home in which to crash over the holidays with the old friends nearby. It was disorienting but may also have been a blessing. If my family still lived in Southold, I might have been tempted to rely on old habits, but instead I had to make a clear break and start a new life. The move preserved many memories in, if not amber, a softer honey.

I didn't go back to visit for years, and when I did, I was joined by my wife, daughter, and friends. I took them to the beautiful beaches, not to relive the past—okay, maybe the first few times—but to enjoy this slice of heaven from a whole new perspective. I saw it fresh and new, and I especially marveled at the wineries cropping up all along the roadside. And like the somewhat show-offy grapevines now stepping to the front, the buildings in town were gradually getting spiffed up.

The library has added a modern new wing, the school building is spreading out, and the supermarket has new shelving. (But the same ominous sign in the parking lot is posted on a fence at the turn-in from Main Street: NOT AN EXIT. NO WAY OUT.) A few practical shops have given way to pricey antique stores, and there's now—you can't stop progress!—a second traffic light. New homes are being built on any bit of land that can't be profitably tilled, but not too many.

Small-town life can be suffocating and limiting, and it can be comforting and liberating. Contrary to popular myth about small towns, everybody did not know everybody's name, but adults felt responsible for kids, no matter whose they were. It was safe to hitchhike at any time of day, and chances are you'd be picked up by a cousin or an uncle of a friend. There were only about two degrees of separation. (We did have the requisite number of spooky homes, shadowy back roads, and sections of woods we just did not go into. And those placid bodies of water did whip up at times, and you did not want to be caught out then.)

Growing up in a city can be limiting, too, not just space-wise, but also in terms of getting a feel for the natural world. You just can't see the sun or moon most of the time, or even the entire shape of any given cloud.

So which is more real, city or country? Neither, and both. What's real is variety, a multitude of experiences, and access to knowledge and the lives of others. In every town are the seeds of a city; in the city there's a different small town outside every door.

We don't get to grow into things as slowly now, neither as kids nor as parents. It's all been accelerated, and the key is to slow it down when possible. Growing up in a small town does that for you. For me at that time, it was a good, safe, fun place to prepare for adulthood and, well, get my feet wet—which, in the summertime, was every single day. Now it takes more than just hopping on a bike to be at the beach, but the extra effort is worth it, as is the conscious effort to keep the outside world at bay at times.

Everyone has a story to tell about a place and a time and lessons learned. This is just my own tiny journey as a child and now a parent. I confess to still being in love with my hometown, fully aware that I've romanticized some of it. I was ready to leave the minute I graduated high school, but I'd move back in a second, and that must mean something.

ACKNOWLEDGMENTS

THIS BOOK IS ALSO DEDICATED TO MY WIFE, JULIE, and my daughter, Savannah, who are my inspiration always. To them my love and admiration and awe.

To our parents, whose unselfishness and unqualified love, then and now, made us who we are . . . thank you so much.

My deep gratitude goes to the first two people to read these "letters" in their early form, and who said, yes, you have good things to say; keep writing: Ruth Liebmann, a longtime business colleague as well as the envy of many of us less smart and funny than she; and Sarah Burnes, my agent and a sea of wise and patient advice. Ruth was the guidance counselor and Sarah the English teacher, shaping the early stages of this book and my perspectives on it.

Shaye Areheart, my editor and publisher, pulled me along to the finish line, helping me get at what I was really trying to say. I knew within ten minutes of meeting her that she would warmly and generously bring this book to its best publication.

Thank you to everyone at Harmony who helped get out the word about this little book, from my longtime friend Philip Patrick to the great publicity team. A huge thanks to the sales representatives who talked it up at bookstores across the country. These unsung heroes have been responsible for kicking off the word-of-mouth on so many books over the years; you'd be amazed at how many books you've read that were once a favorite of a sales rep traveling store to store, talking it up before publication. And thanks to all in design and copyediting who made this book a wonderful object to hold, with all my i's dotted and t's crossed!

To the many friends who encouraged me along the way, thank you so much. And to Jay, my oldest and bestest friend from childhood: I want to be like you if and when I grow up. Really.

To the Phillips Family—Sue, Jim, Alyssa, Kristin, and Connor—our generous weekend neighbors who make summer days such fun, and some winter days, too. (And Jim, thanks for the extra 45's.)

To all my teachers growing up, and to all my daughter's teachers, a huge thank-you. Schoolteachers are as important to our kids' growth and happiness as we are, and there could not be too many awards to be given to today's teachers. In fact, we need more awards and rewards for them, starting with better pay.

acknowledgments

As important as teachers are booksellers and librarians, people who work long hours for not much financial reward, but who go home feeling fulfilled and fortunate if they've reached one new reader that day and thereby changed or improved a life. Truth is, though, that they touch hundreds and hundreds of lives a day.

Thank you to all writers everywhere, particularly the ones who have shaped my view of the world. Your words have all been written before, but your gift is to arrange them in a new, dramatic way, to be the first to see and say something quite that way. You write about what we should know, but have forgotten or have yet to experience. Whether in science fiction or in a mystery, in a children's book or in mature literature, you tell of both the beautiful and the unpleasant, the familiar and the unknown, and we are enlightened by your words. I am an impostor in this world, a pretender, but it was nice visiting.

And last, to go from the lofty to the mundane, a tip of the cup to the coffee bean, and a tip of the glass to the grape. The former gives up its toxin so that at 6 A.M. Saturday and Sunday mornings for a year, before anyone else in the house was up, I could reminisce and write. As for the grape, its juice smooths out the edges after a long day, but more important, its cultivation kept my hometown's farms under till, keeping it much as I remember . . . which sounds selfish, but I want others, kids and adults, to be able to experience what I once had.

ABOUT THE AUTHOR

CARL LENNERTZ has worked in publishing for more than twenty years. He lives in New York City with his wife and daughter. *Cursed by a Happy Childhood* is his first book.